OVERCOMING
LONELINESS

DR. DAVID JEREMIAH

THOMAS NELSON
Since 1798

NASHVILLE   DALLAS   MEXICO CITY   RIO DE JANEIRO

© 1991, 2011 David Jeremiah

Previously published by Here's Life Publishers, Inc. © 1983.

Published in Nashville, Tennessee, by Thomas Nelson. Thomas Nelson is a registered trademark of Thomas Nelson, Inc.

Thomas Nelson, Inc. titles may be purchased in bulk for educational, business, fundraising, or sales promotional use. For information, please e-mail SpecialMarkets@ ThomasNelson.com.

Unless otherwise noted, Scripture quotations are taken from the New King James Version®. © 1982 by Thomas Nelson, Inc. Used by permission. All rights reserved.

Scripture quotations marked NIV are from the Holy Bible, New International Version®, NIV®. © 1978 by the New York International Bible Society. Used by permission of Zondervan Bible Publishers.

Scripture quotations marked KJV are from the King James Version of the Bible.

ISBN 978-0-7852-6076-9 (SE)

Library of Congress Cataloging-in-Publication Data

Jeremiah, David.

Overcoming loneliness / David Jeremiah.
p. cm.
Originally published: San Bernardino, Calif.: Here's Life Publishers, 1983.
Includes bibliographical references.
ISBN 978-0-8407-3356-6 (pbk.)
1. Loneliness—Religious aspects—Christianity.
2. Consolation. I. Title.
IBV4911.J47 19921
248.8'6—dc20
91-39960

Printed in the United States of America

11 12 13 14 15 QG 5 4 3 2 1

Contents

Chapter 1

Loneliness—A Disease of Our Time

They are crammed and jammed in buses, but each of them's alone.[1]

I n recent years, more people than ever before are speaking of overwhelming loneliness. Even though there are more and more people in our world, living closer together, rubbing elbows at every turn, many have fewer and fewer meaningful personal relationships. For some, the isolation, which they feel even in a crowd, is devastating.

A study released in the American Sociological Review in 2006 reported that the number of people who say they have no one to confide in nearly tripled between 1985 and 2004. Relationship networks have shrunk. A social shift has taken place, and fewer people are creating ties in the community and neighborhood and, instead, limiting their conversation inside the home with their spouse or close family member. While family relationships are important, isolating oneself from community can be very lonely, especially if something happens to that spouse or parent.[2]

Craig Ellison, in reporting on statistical studies, says, "A fourth of the people questioned in one survey said they felt very lonely or cut off from other people at some time during the preceding weeks." In another study, according to Ellison, 27 percent of the unmarried women, 10 percent of the married women, 23 percent of the unmarried men, and 6 percent of married men expressed intense loneliness. "Almost half the widows over fifty living in one metropolitan area said that loneliness was their worst problem. Loneliest of all, researchers find, are elderly men, who live alone and are infirm."[3]

When *People* magazine conducted a survey and asked the question, "What is the connection between loneliness and health?" one respondent replied, "That's like asking what is the connection between *air* and one's health."[4] Just as we can't live without the air we breathe, we can't survive without human companionship. When we're deprived of it, we experience loneliness—the feeling of being isolated—and it takes a tremendous toll. Specialists say that social isolation, the sudden loss of love, and chronic loneliness contribute significantly to illness and even to premature death.

All these factors suggest that loneliness may well be the disease of our time. We need to talk about it, understand why we experience it, and find ways to overcome it.

What exactly is loneliness? Some describe it in physical terms.

- It's an empty feeling in the pit of the stomach, almost to the point of nausea.
- It's an underlying anxiety, a big black pit.
- It's a sharp ache in moments of grief or separation.
- It's a long period of stress that wears you down until you're discouraged and defeated.
- It's a longing for completeness.

One author says that loneliness "is always characterized by an empty feeling somewhere in the region of the diaphragm . . . It is a craving to be filled. And at various times we seek to fill this vacuum with everything from food to alcohol to endless demands on other people. Or we will try to pacify it—by using drugs or just going to sleep—or perhaps we will attempt to escape from it."[5]

No anguish is like the anguish of loneliness. I am aware of this anguish in letters that come to my desk from prisoners. I hear it in the voice of a woman who calls to tell me her husband has left her. I see it in the face of a man who has just buried his wife. I ache with its effects as I hug and try to comfort grandparents and parents at the funeral of a beautiful child who was snatched from them in just a few hours by a violent disease.

I observe the cruelty of it in the faces of single people

who are trying to find community and fellowship in a religious and social world that is family-oriented and couple-centered. I see it in teenagers who are making the transition from childhood to adulthood: Everything is changing; they feel their parents don't understand, and they're all alone with the strangeness. I see it in my wife's eyes when the ministry to which God has called us separates us for many nights in a row.

I hear the sounds of loneliness in songs such as "Without You," "I'm so Lonely I Could Die," "Ballad of a Lonely Man," and "Eleanor Rigby." They all seem to say, "All the lonely people—where do they all come from?"

Katherine Barrett has part of the answer: "In a society where most people live in impersonal cities or suburbs, where electronic entertainment often replaces one-to-one conversation, where people move from job to job, and state to state, and marriage to marriage, loneliness has become an epidemic."[6]

Even though loneliness is a modern day epidemic, it isn't a new phenomenon. Do you remember the lament of the Ancient Mariner?

> Alone, alone, all, all alone,
> Alone on a wide, wide sea!
> And never a saint took pity on
> My soul in agony.[7]

Even King David knew loneliness. He said, "No one cares for my soul" (Psalms 142:4). The lives of thousands of people are summarized in those words. *No one cares.* Is that the way it is? Is that the way it should be?

In his book *The Devil's Advocate*, Morris West writes: "Let me tell you something important. It is no new thing to be lonely. It comes to all of us sooner or later. Friends die, family dies, lovers and husband, too. We get old; we get sick. The last and greatest loneliness is death. There are no pills to cure that. There are no formulas to make it go away. It is a [human] condition we cannot escape, and if we try to run from it we are driven to a darker hell than the one we experience in the midst of it. But if we face it, we remember that there are a million others like us and if we reach out to comfort them and not ourselves, we discover in the end that we are lonely no longer, for we are in a new family, the family of man."[8]

I believe Christians can go one step further. Not only are we in the family of man, "we are in the family of God." We have the "reassurance that God wants to meet us in our loneliness, and we will find that, with His help, we can overcome it."

Q. How do you feel when you are lonely?

Q. How can you overcome this lonely feeling?

Q. People are sometimes lonely—even in a family setting. What type of activities might they do to overcome their loneliness?

Q. How can you help someone overcome loneliness?

Q. How can God help us with our loneliness?

Q. Is it possible to feel lonely in a crowd? Why would that be?

Q. How can we use the family of God to help us cope with our loneliness?

Q. Katherine Barrett says loneliness is an epidemic. List the lonely people you know and possible ways you can help them.

Chapter 2

Lonely Saints

I'm alone Lord
alone
a thousand miles from home.
There's no one here who knows my
name
except the clerk
and he spelled it wrong,
no one to eat dinner with
laugh at my jokes
listen to my gripes
be happy with me about what happened
today
and say that's great.
No one cares.
There's just this lousy bed
and slush in the street outside
between the buildings.
I feel sorry for myself
and I've plenty of reason to.
Maybe I ought to say

I'm on top of it
praise the Lord
things are great
but they're not.
Tonight
it's all
gray slush.[1]

Every year during football season a lot of Americans spend many enjoyable hours with their favorite team. And then the season's over. It's gone. There's a letdown and a feeling of loss.

That's a picture of life, isn't it? The things that have no eternal value, but are just temporal—they go, they end, and only a kind of emptiness is left when it's all over.

Things of eternal value don't leave that feeling. Our relationship with the Lord never leaves an empty feeling. In Jesus Christ we find rest, joy, and happiness regardless of whether or not something happens or whether our teams win.

People face different kinds of loneliness. A particular kind of loneliness comes to us when we have lost a loved one. It touches us at the very core of our lives. Some readers of this book have recently lost someone in their immediate families—a husband, a wife, a child, a grandparent—and an aching loneliness is in their hearts because of it.

Separation from friends causes loneliness too. Missionaries often speak of that. They know what it's like to be on the other side of the world, facing crises, with no one there to help. Nobody is close enough to them to understand what they're experiencing.

Another kind of loneliness can take place when you're with others—in the midst of a large crowd or even when you're surrounded by people you love. The feeling that no one cares creeps in and you crave affirmation from someone that you matter.

Christians are sometimes called upon to take positions that are unpopular, that do not meet with the approval of the majority. We feel very much alone then, and because of these experiences we can identify with a man in the Bible who for fifty years carried on a public ministry that was not appreciated.

Jeremiah, God's prophet through the reign of five different kings, watched terrible things happen to those to whom God had called him to minister. The first few verses of his prophecy, the Old Testament Book of Jeremiah, identify the three major kings under whom he served: Josiah, Jehoiakim, and Zedekiah. Two other men were king for only three months each. During this time period, Jeremiah watched disorder on a national level because of political upheaval and corrupt leadership. He saw disturbing social problems and dissension tear his people apart. Discontent and despair seemed to be the mood of the times. But Jeremiah continued to minister as a prophet of God in the land of Judah, no matter how unpopular, opposed, condemned, ridiculed, and scorned he was.

On one occasion he was stoned and thrown out of his home town. On another occasion he was disgraced and beaten in public. Another time he was imprisoned, and once he was thrown into a pit and left for dead. Eventually he wrote *Lamentations*, a book of poetry often called a collection of funeral poems. They are the outpouring of his grief at the destruction of the holy city. Because of them he has been called the "weeping prophet." If you haven't read Lamentations recently, read it and you'll come to know and understand a lonely, hurting man.

Jeremiah ministered during the last years of Judah's history, from the thirteenth year of King Josiah until the destruction of the nation. The decline of Judah greatly depressed him. He said,

> *An astonishing and horrible thing*
> *Has been committed in the land:*
> *The prophets prophesy falsely,*
> *And the priests rule by their own power,*
> *And my people love to have it so.*
>
> (Jeremiah 5:30–31)

The prophets were not speaking from God, the priests were using their sacred mission for personal gain, and the people didn't object. That kind of corruption was to their fancy.

Jeremiah looked out over his nation and saw a whole generation of backslidden people who had fallen away from their godly moorings. They had walked a road away from God. "The harvest is past," he said. "The summer is ended, and we are not saved!" (Jeremiah 8:20). As he looked at the awful apathy among the people who were supposed to be God's people, depression swept his soul.

One of the key words in the Book of Jeremiah is *backslide*. Over and over again, Jeremiah mentions the backsliding of God's people. For example,

> *Your own wickedness will correct you,*
> *And your backslidings will reprove you.*
> *Know therefore and see it is an evil and*
> *   bitter thing.* (2:19)

The Lord said also to me in the days of Josiah the king: "Have you seen what backsliding Israel has done?" (3:6)

Then I saw that for all the causes for which backsliding Israel had committed adultery, I had put her away. (3:8)

Return, you backsliding children, And I will heal your backslidings. (3:22)

Jeremiah cried out against all this, but his cries fell on deaf ears. These people had lifted apathy and indifference to new heights.

Lord Macaulay, who was a British historian, wrote

these words about somebody else, but they fit the man Jeremiah. He said: "It is difficult to conceive any situation more painful than that of a great man, condemned to watch the lingering agony of an exhausted country, to tend it during the alternating fits of stupefaction and raving which preceded its dissolution, and to see the symptoms of vitality disappear one by one until nothing is left but coldness and darkness and corruption."[2]

Just as this man did with his country, Jeremiah stood in the nation he loved, among the people to whom God had called him, and watched the awful moral decline that ultimately placed the people in captivity. Jeremiah went to his grave having seen the death of his nation.

It is one thing to watch a nation fall; it's another to watch its people be totally insensitive to the inevitable. It was the disinterest of the people that broke Jeremiah's heart. He grieved about their sad spiritual state and spent a great deal of time weeping.

> *Oh, that my head were waters,*
> *And my eyes a fountain of tears,*
> *That I might weep day and night*
> *For the slain of the daughter of my people!*
>
> (9:1)

> *But if you will not hear it,*
> *My soul will weep in secret for your pride.*
>
> (13:17)

Let my eyes flow with tears night and day,
And let them not cease;
For the virgin daughter of my people
Has been broken with a mighty stroke, with a very
*   severe blow.* (14:17)

In the Book of Lamentations we find instance after instance of Jeremiah weeping for a nation that had been reared on the precepts of God and had turned from them. God had raised him up, made him a prophet to pronounce God's judgment and the way of deliverance, but the people would not listen. Their ears were closed; they refused to hear. As Jeremiah thought about that in the night watches, loneliness overwhelmed him. He was alone, deserted and friendless, God's representative in a decadent society. The desertion of his friends distressed him.

See, O Lord, that I am in distress;
My soul is troubled . . .
They have heard that I sigh,
With no one to comfort me.
All my enemies have heard of my trouble;
They are glad that You have done it.

                    (Lamentations 1:20–21)

I did not sit in the assembly of the mockers,
Nor did I rejoice;
I sat alone because of Your hand,
For You have filled me with indignation.

Why is my pain perpetual
And my wound incurable,
Which refuses to be healed?

(Jeremiah 15:17–18)

Jeremiah felt what all of us are prone to feel in such situations. He was ready to disown it all. He had what we call in the modern vernacular his own, private pity party. And thinking back over what we've already learned about this lonely man, we cannot really blame him; from the human standpoint, he wanted to die. He was ready to quit. He was all by himself, and you can feel the ache of his heart as he writes. Each of us has had some kind of experience at one time or another, an experience with isolation, and can imagine how Jeremiah felt. I don't know what finally was the last blow, but one day Jeremiah decided he had had enough; all of it was too much for him.

Cursed be the day in which I was born!
Let the day not be blessed in which my mother
  bore me!
Let the man be cursed
Who brought news to my father, saying,
"A male child has been born to you!"
Making him very glad.
And let that man be like the cities
Which the Lord overthrew, and did not relent;
Let him hear the cry in the morning

And the shouting at noon,

Because he did not kill me from the womb.

That my mother might have been my grave,

And her womb always enlarged with me,

Why did I come forth from the womb to see labor
and sorrow,

That my days should be consumed with shame?

(Jeremiah 20:14–18)

Jeremiah was so distraught he wished he had never been born; He had hit bottom and didn't want to go on.

Someone wrote a paraphrase of these verses. I don't know who it was, but he must have been a modern-day pastor writing on a Monday morning. It vividly expresses Jeremiah's despair: "I had no idea when you called me into Your office that it would be like this. I pictured myself preaching great sermons, perhaps working a miracle now and then. I foresaw some opposition, but I thought I would override it in calm victory. You never mentioned my destruction or the number of those who would despise me. You neglected to mention that everyone in Jerusalem would mock me constantly. I'm the laughing stock of all Judah! Everyone points or smirks or laughs or snarls at me when I walk down the street, even the smallest children. I *quit!*"[3]

Do you ever talk like that? Have you ever said, "I quit!" Then you can understand Jeremiah, He wanted to disown the whole thing. Everyone at one time or another has wanted to quit.

Oh, that I had in the wilderness
A lodging place for travelers;
That I might leave my people,
And go from them!
For they are all adulterers,
An assembly of treacherous men.

(Jeremiah 9:2)

What was Jeremiah saying? "I wish I had a motel room in the wilderness so that I could get away from this hassle. If I did, I'd do it tomorrow. If I could just get in my car and drive away from it all, leave it behind me, oh, what a good feeling that would be!"

Do you ever feel like that? James Conway, in his book *Men in Mid-Life Crisis*, speaks of how he sometimes feels as a pastor, husband, and father. He feels stretched to the breaking point, unable to satisfy all the demands put on him. He doesn't have the same reasons for his despair as Jeremiah, but his loneliness and longing for relief are just as genuine. He also, from time to time, wants to quit.

I feel like a vending machine, dispensing products. Someone pushes a button, and out comes a sermon. Someone punches another button for a solution to a personal or administrative problem. The family pushes buttons, and out comes dollars or time involvement. The community pushes other buttons, and I show up at meetings, sign petitions, and take stands. It is easy for a man . . . to feel that he is trapped with obligations to everyone, and the frustration is that he can't get out.[4]

Jeremiah wanted to quit, but he didn't. He was faithful to what God had called him to do. For fifty years he stayed by the stuff, so to speak, not appreciated. Nobody came by and said, "Boy, it's tremendous what you're doing to save our nation." But, though he had his low moments, though he wanted to run, he was faithful.

I'm glad the Bible has recorded his emotions. Reading his words and knowing his emotions makes us feel better about our own. Knowing that a man of the Bible felt complete despair and overwhelming loneliness puts our feelings in perspective. Some people say the Bible paints plastic men, straw people, but it doesn't. It shows them the way they were: real flesh and blood individuals whose feelings sound a lot like ours.

What Jeremiah did, you and I can do. The things that were true in his life can be true in our lives. How did he do it? Four stabilizing factors kept Jeremiah secure and at the task to which God had called him. These four concrete principles caused him to be victorious.

First, *he had a conviction of his calling*. Did I say conviction? Well, at first he said, "Okay, it seems like no matter what I do, whenever I open my mouth, somebody doesn't like it. I'll tell you what—I'm not even going to talk. I'll just be quiet. I know when to shut up. I won't even mention the Lord's name." That's what he wanted to do, but his conviction was too great. He couldn't be quiet.

> *But His word was in my heart like a*
> > *burning fire*
> *Shut up in my bones;*
> *I was weary of holding it back*
> *And I could not.*
>
> > (Jeremiah 20:9)

How did he get such conviction? He came to the realization that God had called him. If you look carefully at the first chapter of Jeremiah, you will understand why that call was such an important part of his life.

> *Then the word of the Lord came to me, saying:*
> *"Before I formed you in the womb I knew you;*
> *Before you were born I sanctified you;*
> *I ordained you a prophet to the nations."*
>
> > (Jeremiah 1:4–5)

These verses tell us four things about his calling. God *knew* Jeremiah before he was formed; God *formed* Jeremiah in the womb; God *sanctified* Jeremiah and set him apart for His service; God *ordained* Jeremiah. God said, "You're my man, Jeremiah; you do it." Even his name, Jeremiah, carries out God's command. It means literally "whom Jehovah appoints." Jeremiah realized that he was an appointed servant called by God. In the midst of the discouragements of his life and the problems of his society, the thing that held him in place and kept him going was the realization that he was where God wanted him and doing what God wanted. Though he didn't understand the circumstances, He was convicted about his calling. He couldn't quit.

When I was considering going into the ministry, my father said, "David, if you can do anything else, do it." That was rather strange advice for a man to give his son, I thought, when I knew he'd been praying all his life that I'd be a preacher. What he meant was if my call to the ministry was not so strong as to blot out all desire for any other vocation, when trouble came, as it surely would, I would vacillate. I would want to quit. He was telling me to be sure of my calling, to be convicted about it.

My father's advice does not apply only to those who would be pastors. It applies to everyone no matter what God has commissioned us to do. For instance, some of you may be college students who face financial difficulty and academic pressure. You could be thinking about how great it would be to have a job so that you could earn money and do the things you want to do. The pressure is on, and you want to quit. But if you really believe God called you to go to school, you won't quit.

Every person has a calling from God—every one of us. Whatever yours is, you'd better be sure of it. If you know that's where God has put you, it will help you when tough times come.

So reason number one for Jeremiah's steadfastness

when he wanted to quit was his *conviction of his calling.* He wanted to get out, but something in him drove him on. That something was the knowledge that God had put him in that place, given him a job to do, and implanted His word in him.

The second principle that gave Jeremiah victory was, he had *confidence in his companion.*

> *For I heard many mocking:*
> *"Fear on every side!"*
> *"Report," they say, "and we will report it!"*
> *All my acquaintances watched for my*
>   *stumbling, saying,*
> *"Perhaps he can be induced;*
> *Then we will prevail against him,*
> *And we will take our revenge on him."*
> But the Lord is with me as a mighty,
>   awesome One.
> *Therefore my persecutors will stumble, and*
>   *will not prevail.*
>   (Jeremiah 20:10–11, emphasis added)

Jeremiah said, "I know they're after me. I know even my friends are trying to get me. But I've got the Lord; He's my companion."

Do you remember what Jeremiah said when God asked him to go into the ministry? He said, "Lord, I can't do it. I'm a child. I'm not mature enough." But the Lord answered his objection with these words: "Do not be afraid of their faces, for I am with you to deliver you. . . . They will fight against you, but they shall not prevail against you. For I am with you." (Jeremiah 1:8, 19)

Just like Jeremiah, we need companionship. We need fellowship. God has built these needs into us. It isn't true that all we'll ever need throughout our lives is Jesus. We need the companionship of other people too. But in those moments when we are between friends, in those dark caverns of being all alone, we have the Master Companion who stays with us through it all.

> *Now, thus says the Lord, who created you, O Jacob,*
> *And He who formed you, O Israel:*
> *"Fear not, for I have redeemed you;*
> *I have called you by your name; You are Mine.*
> *When you pass through the waters, I will be with you;*
> *And through the rivers, they shall not overflow you.*
> *When you walk through the fire, you shall not*
>   *be burned,*
> *Nor shall the flame scorch you.*
> *For I am the Lord your God,*
> *The Holy One of Israel, your Savior."*
> (Isaiah 43:1–3)

The third principle is that Jeremiah had a *commitment that went beyond his circumstances.*

> *Blessed is the man who trusts in the Lord,*
> *And whose hope is the Lord.*

> *For he shall be like a tree planted by the waters,*
> *Which spreads out its roots by the river,*
> *And will not fear when heat comes,*
> *But its leaf will be green,*
> *And will not be anxious in the year of drought,*
> *Nor will cease from yielding fruit.*
>
> (Jeremiah 17:7–8)

When you put your roots down deep in trust in God, when your faith is in Him, your confidence goes beyond the circumstances.

How many Christians vacillate with the circumstances? Jeremiah said, "In the midst of all these problems and troubles and difficulties, my trust is in the Lord. It doesn't matter whether it's summer or winter or what. I don't need to be anxious because I have a commitment that goes beyond these circumstances."

Do you have that kind of commitment? Or are you in the everyday hassle so many people experience—up and down, up and down in reaction to circumstances?

> And let us not grow weary while doing good, for in
> due season we shall reap if we do not lose heart.
>
> (Galatians 6:9)

> *He who continually goes forth weeping,*
> *Bearing seed for sowing,*
> *Shall doubtless come again with rejoicing,*
> *Bringing his sheaves with him.* (Psalms 126:6)

Be steadfast, immovable, always abounding in the work
of the Lord, knowing that your labor is not in vain in
the Lord.

(1 Corinthians 15:58)

Someone has said, "Integrity is carrying out a commitment even after the circumstances in which it was made
have changed." Have a conviction of your calling, confidence in your companion, and a commitment beyond
your circumstances.

Finally, Jeremiah had a *chorus of celebration*.

Sing to the Lord! Praise the Lord!
For He has delivered the life of the poor
From the hand of evildoers.

(Jeremiah 20:13)

How could a person in a situation like Jeremiah's possibly
sing to the Lord? He did it with faith.

Doctors speak of the "threshold of pain," the level of
awareness at which a person feels pain. Some people have a
high threshold; others have a very low threshold. When you
take an aspirin, it has no effect on your physical problem. All
it does is raise your pain threshold so that you must experience more pain before you are aware of it. The aspirin makes
you feel better because you don't feel how bad you feel.

Joy is like that. Happiness and joy are spiritual aspirin.
When you are filled with the joy of the Lord, the hurts
around you don't touch you so quickly.

I have found that psychologically, music raises my threshold of pain. On days when I am discouraged, I'll go home, turn on the stereo, and begin to listen to music. God uses that to assuage my soul and bring me out of pain. Is it any wonder that Saul required David to come and play for him on the harp to bring him out of his depression? That's what music can do in our hearts.

Medical specialists have now established that feelings of joy raise the threshold of pain. A delightful book by Norman Cousins, called *The Anatomy of an Illness as Perceived by the Patient*, was on the best seller list. It is Cousins' story. He was told he had one chance in five hundred to live and decided to make the most of his life. In effect he said, "If I'm going to die, I don't want to die in surroundings like these." He left the hospital and rented a hotel room, a plush hotel room, and began laughing. He secured tapes of some old "Candid Camera" TV shows along with other humorous films and watched those comedies every two hours from morning till night. And he began to get better.[5] He demonstrated the truth of the Old Testament statement: "A merry heart doeth good like a medicine" (Proverbs 17:22 KJV). Many times, the joy of praise and thanksgiving to God will dissipate the hurt you feel, for, as Ezra said, "The joy of the Lord is your strength" (Nehemiah 8:10).

Are you joyful? Do you have anything you're praising God for? I learned a long time ago that there is always something for which I can give thanks. On the very worst day I still can be glad about something.

The principle of the power of joy is demonstrated in the story of Anne Frank. Perhaps you recall that Anne and her family were prisoners in their home during the Second World War. They suffered greatly with unimaginable hardship and difficulty. Anne kept a diary of their experience, recording the fear of discovery they lived with every day. But along with the descriptions of the danger and despair, Anne recorded the feelings in her heart. Somehow, despite the suffering, she found joy. In 1944, when she was a young girl, she wrote, "Nearly every evening I go to the attic, and from my favorite spot on the floor, I look up at the blue sky. As long as this exists, I thought, and I may live to see it—this sunshine, the cloudless skies—while this lasts, I cannot be unhappy. Riches can all be lost, but that happiness in your own heart can only be veiled."[6]

We have something more than blue sky and clouds. We have Jesus Christ living in us. Though the world may crumble around us, He is the blue sky; He is the light from on high that thrills and encourages our hearts. I can look beyond my circumstances into the face of the one who loves me more than I know, the one who would never allow me to go through anything that is not for my own good. And I say to myself, and to you, be convicted of your calling, have confidence in your companion, be committed, sing a chorus of celebration.

And don't quit.

Q. What were the problems Jeremiah encountered?

Q. How did Jeremiah overcome these problems?

Q. Can you apply what happened to Jeremiah to your own experiences?

Q. What would you say is the best cure for unhappiness?

Q. How can you obtain and keep a good mental attitude?

Q. In the face of adversity, it is hard to feel positive. What activities make you feel positive?

Q. Who can you turn to for help? Remember, you always have the Lord.

Q. How can you follow the example of Jeremiah?

Q. How did Jeremiah deal with the socio-political problems he faced?

Q. What or who is the key to happiness?

Chapter 3

Lonely Singles

God,
it's a new year's eve
and i took a hot bath
and poured powder and lotion
and perfume recklessly,
and donned my newest
long, dainty
nightgown.
i guess i was hoping
all that would erase
the agony of being
alone
in such a gallant,
celebrating,
profound moment
when everyone so likes
to be with someone
to watch
a new year in.

it hasn't helped
too much.
I've tried to sleep
hoping that would beat
away the endless hours, but
after all afternoon and two hours
tonight, I'm worn out from sleep.
I've stumbled from one room to the next,
wanting to cry . . .
O God,
the walls are so silent . . .
and there is no one around
to laugh and change the subject . . .
I so wish for a friend's lap,
to bury my head
and let my tears spill
unabashedly and free . . . [1]

One of the great phenomena of our day is what sociologists call "the singles' explosion." Between 1970 and 1982, the number of single adults who had never been married grew from 10.9 million to 19.4 million, a seventy-eight percent increase.[2] As of 2009, according to the US Census Bureau, this number has skyrocketed to 58.9 million. The same study shows that 31.7 million adults live alone; meaning twenty-seven percent of American households were run by one person, a ten percent increase over 1970. Part of this phenomenon is that there are 11.6 million single parents living with their children. If we include all single people (the widowed and divorced as well as the never married), the result is that there are 96.6 million single people in the United States.

Nearly one-third of all households in the United States consists of a person living alone.[3] The real estate industry has reacted to this trend by building an increasing number of condominiums for singles only. Smaller houses are being built, with fewer rooms, reflecting the needs of this segment of our population.

The need of singles for satisfying relationships has caused the proliferation of many enterprises: singles' bars, for example, encounter and support groups, and computerized dating services. A Christian newspaper once carried an ad that urged singles to subscribe to a monthly publication through which they can meet other singles on four continents. The ad began, "God did not ordain singleness and loneliness." It is partially correct. God does not ordain loneliness.

"I sit in the pew next to a warm body every week, but I feel no heat," said one older woman. "I'm in the faith, but I draw no active love. I sing hymns with those next to me, but I hear only my own voice. When the service is finished, I leave just as I came in—hungry for someone to touch me, to tell me that I'm a person worth something to someone. Just a smile would do it, or perhaps a gesture—some sign that I am not a stranger."

This woman speaks of the kind of loneliness that could be dispelled in many ways. She needs affirmation of her worth. She needs relationships with people.

Oh, Father, I just need a reason to go on. It's getting' dark; Father; I'm afraid. This reminds me of another dark place I knew; I was three years stumbling through it. Not again, Father; please!

I hurt. Inside I am screaming. I do not want this. One by one you have taken away the people I depended on. Now only You are left. I do not want to trust You—You who have taken away all that mattered. But I am too tired to fight You anymore.

Would You hold my hand, please? It's getting darker. Too dark now to see more than a step ahead. And colder too. You know, You don't talk to me like people do. I guess that's what I miss. And people are tangible. I can feel them there.

It's all black now, Father. It looks to me like it will never be right again. Not here. But when we get to Your place, that's bright again isn't it?

It's hard to accept this blackness for that long. But I guess You're not asking me to. Only to accept it for now, this present minute. It's just that these minutes run together 'til I can hardly remember a time before them.[4]

These poignant cries for help would not necessarily be satisfied by a marriage partner. And appropriately, these lonely people understand that. Marriage is not a guarantee that loneliness will end, even though many think it is.

In 1 Corinthians we learn that God is not confused (as a lot of us are) about the subject of singleness.

> Now for the matters you wrote about: It is good for a man not to marry. (7:1 NIV)

> I wish that all men were as I am. But each man has his own gift from God; one has this gift, another has that. Now to the unmarried and the widows I say: It is good for them to stay unmarried, as I am. But if they cannot control themselves, they should marry, for it is better to marry than to burn with passion.
>
> (7:7–9 NIV)

> I would like you to be free from concern. An unmarried man is concerned about the Lord's affairs—how he can please the Lord. But a married man is concerned about the affairs of this world—how he can please his wife—and his interests are divided. An unmarried woman or virgin is concerned about the Lord's affairs: Her aim is to be devoted to the Lord in both body and spirit. But a married woman is concerned about the affairs of this world—how she can please her husband. I am saying this for your own good, not to restrict you, but that you may live in a right way in undivided devotion to the Lord.
>
> (7:32–35 NIV)

In this passage as well as elsewhere in the Bible, God says five things to singles: Acknowledge your singleness, accept singleness as God's gift, allow yourself to grow, activate your singleness, and affirm your singleness with gratitude. These are important principles for you to understand and appreciate, particularly if you are lonely and feel it is because you are single.

Acknowledge Your Singleness

Three times in 1 Corinthians 7 we read that is it good to be single (see verses 1, 8, and 26). Why is that so startling? Well, most singles have been made to feel that to be single is to be second class. The following letter vividly expresses how many singles feel.

> Dear Pastor:
>
> I too am single—never been married—and I really believe some couples and elderly people don't realize the hurt and grief they sometimes inflict on people like me. I often get questions and comments like: "What's a sweet girl like you doing single?" "God has just the right man somewhere." "Maybe a friend's wife will die!" "What's wrong with you?" "When are you getting married?" "Maybe your standards are too high." "I prayed for my husband; all you have to do is pray."
>
> Why can't people be more sensitive? Everything in this world seems geared to couples. Even churches

have Valentine's Day banquets, Christmas banquets, overnight camping trips, retreats, etc. Everything revolves around husband and wife, parent, child, and teen.

I know there are advantages to being single, but if one more person tells me how cheap it is to live singly, I think I'll scream. They don't realize that we singles have just as many bills and payments as do those who have husband, wife, or family.

We need to remember that God said it is *good* to be single.

Accept Singleness as a Gift from God

"Are you kidding? A gift from God? You bring me a man, and then we'll talk about God's gift." These are the words one unmarried woman said to me, and they reveal her despair. They show she feels cheated, unfulfilled, different. Another woman poetically described the kind of gift she hopes to receive from God.

Unknown Man

> *Oh, unknown man, whose rib I am, why don't you*
> *come for me?*
> *A lonely, homesick rib I am that would with others be.*
> *I want to wed—there, now 'tis said!*
> *(I won't deny and fib.)*
> *I want my man to come at once and claim his rib!*

Some men have thought that I'd be theirs,
    but only for a bit,
We found out soon it wouldn't do—
    we didn't seem to fit.
There's just one place, the only space I'll fit
    (I will not fib),
I want my man to come at once and claim
    his rib.[5]

But Paul said, "I wish that all men were even as I myself. But each one has his own gift from God, one in this manner and another in that" (1 Corinthians 7:7). Being married is a gift of God, but God also gives the gift of being single.

In *The Living Bible* this passage continues, "God gives some the gift of a husband or wife, and [to] others he gives the gift of being able to stay happily unmarried." And Jesus said, "For there are eunuchs who were born thus from their mother's womb, and there are eunuchs who were made eunuchs by men, and there are eunuchs who have made themselves eunuchs for the kingdom of heaven's sake. He who is able to accept it, let him accept it" (Matthew 19:12).

People are single for four kinds of reasons: physical, medical, and spiritual, or they just want to be single— not everybody wants to be married and apparently that is a part of God's plan. Some of the greatest people who ever served God were single. Rejoice in all the gifts God has given you, including your singleness.

Allow Your Singleness to Be a Source of Growth

Seeking marriage is not wrong, but don't let that search dominate your life. We must not make finding a marriage partner the supreme goal of our lives by putting all our energies into searching for a mate. We must learn to be in God's will. A very wise person said, "There is something far worse than single loneliness, and that is marital misery." Learn contentment, for it is great gain.

If God has a mate for you, He knows how to bring the two of you together. Don't take things into your own hands. I think the young woman who wrote the following note to me understood this truth:

> Basically I'm content with being single, but I do hope the Lord has marriage in my future. Personally, I'd rather be married than single. For now, though, I know the Lord loves me, and I know He has me single. Trusting in Him, waiting on Him and His plan, is difficult. But I know that He is my rock, and that's more important to me than being married. Please pray that each day there will be more of Christ in my life.

Wherever you are, whatever your situation, use the time to grow both mentally and spiritually.

Activate Your Singleness for God

A person who doesn't have the stress and strain of marital life is more free to devote his or her full energies to God. But a person with a family is, as Paul said, concerned with the affairs of the world. Priorities become more of a problem. A man came to his pastor and said, "My wife has left me." "When did it happen?" the pastor asked. The man replied, "Well, I don't know for sure. It was sometime between Monday and Friday . . . I've been at church every night this week."

There's not a Christian man or woman who wholeheartedly loves God who doesn't struggle with priorities. How much time belongs to God? How much time belongs to others? How can all of us—single or married—balance these priorities to please the Lord? That's the kind of struggle we ought to be involved in. If we are married, the family is a priority in God's economy, and each child adds a new dimension of responsibility. I have no right to serve the Lord as a minister of the Gospel and neglect my home and family. But Paul's point is: If you're not married and you don't have a family, you can give yourself totally to God without the pressure of those relationships. You can be totally consumed with serving God.

If you are single you may say, "What in the world does that have to do with my loneliness?" Well, it has everything to do with your loneliness. Single people who are lonely are people who are worrying about what isn't happening to them instead of finding out what they could be doing to minister to others. Activating your singleness for God can bring you great blessings, and your loneliness will recede until it is a dim memory.

Pastor, there have been many compensations for being single. How many husbands would have put up with the many midnight—or 1:00, 2:00, 3:00 in the morning—phone calls I have received from my hurting friends. Many times I have gotten dressed and gone out in the middle of the night for a cup of coffee with a friend who was hurting.

I'm so glad that God has used me in this small way. I place a high premium on my availability to other people. There are many verses that give me encouragement every day, but a special one is Romans 8:32: "He that spared not His own Son, but delivered Him up for us all, how shall He not with Him also freely give us all things?" Right now, His freely giving me all things does not include a husband. How dare I believe that God has made a mistake in His plan for my life?

It's okay to be single. God has a special plan for you. That plan includes reaching out and helping others. The answer to your need and aloneness—your feeling that you're not a part of what's going on—is not to wait until somebody gives to you but to keep giving yourself. You'll discover that when you serve God, your own needs begin to be met. It works whatever your marital status.

Affirm Your Singleness with Gratitude

One thing I've learned in studying loneliness is that the supreme solution is a spirit of thanksgiving. It's hard to be lonely when you're thankful because giving thanks means taking spiritual inventory of your blessings. You realize that although you may be physically alone, God has done many good things to minister to your needs. When we consciously take inventory of our blessings, sometimes we are surprised at what they are:

> I was happily married for twenty-four years and praise God for those years. I've been single for five years now (not by choice). I hadn't thought of it as a "blessing" until you brought it to my attention. Why is it a blessing? Because I have been closer to the Lord than ever before in my life.

One young divorcee has found the way from loneliness to service and describes her journey this way:

> Financial, emotional, and family stress are among the many areas the Lord has helped me to deal with as a single parent. A heart of thanksgiving is the answer to overcoming depression and loneliness.
>
> One particular area was extremely difficult for me to cope with. It is probable that other singles (particularly those who are widowed or divorced) experience this difficulty but are unwilling to talk

about it, especially with a pastor. Because sex is so personal, many people are hesitant to discuss it. But the Lord has given me victory in this area. I hope my sharing it with you will enable you to counsel others.

My divorce was a painful time. During the ten years of my marriage, my husband and I enjoyed a loving and fulfilling sexual relationship. At the time of our divorce, I felt an extreme need for physical contact, but I also felt that the Lord did not want me to seek a physical relationship. On my own steam, I tried to overcome my natural desires and failed continually. My efforts only produced more frustration.

After much struggle, I searched the Scriptures for a biblical answer to my frustration. I was reminded by Philippians 4:19 that my God will supply all my needs. God created me; He knows me better than anyone. I had a need to be held and hugged. It was more than a desire—it was a need. I prayed and asked God to help me and to meet my needs.

The next morning I received a telephone call requesting that I teach four-year-olds during the eight o'clock hour. The following Sunday morning was filled with hugs and kisses and an outpouring of God's love. The Lord has met my needs through the love of those children. Sunday morning is the highlight of my week.

Some parents are so concerned that their daughters and sons marry into a higher social circle that they will sacrifice (usually it's the kids who make the sacrifice) to get them into "good" marriages. But that is not the way we should approach marriage. The attitude that Paul develops in 1 Corinthians 7 is the attitude of praise for wherever we (or our children) are. At the end of the chapter, he speaks to widows and says, "Maybe it's the best if you not remarry. But praise God for it—be happy in that situation!" (See verses 39–40.).

I think God says to us that we can lift our eyes to heaven and say, "Lord, I don't understand why I'm where I am. But I'm in Your will; I'm in Your plan; I praise You for where I am. Use me right here to glorify Your name, to honor You and be a blessing to other people, and to be thankful."

A young single man who has internalized the truth of God's Word understands where he is:

Let me share a few things that I believe were given to me by my Father in heaven. He has taught me this in my experience as a single person.

Number one: Singles have a lot of love to give away, so give it! What I receive is usually somewhat proportionate to what I give. The biggest share of a blessing comes from my giving, not from my receiving.

Number two: The need to belong is responded to by my willingness to commit myself to something—to be vulnerable: to God, to a ministry, to a group, to a friend. I often make the mistake of shying away from committing myself, and when I do, I feel as if I don't belong.

Number three: Realize that loneliness is not always bad. In fact, on occasion it may be the very thing that draws me toward God. There is nothing that will bring me to my knees more quickly than feeling totally alone in difficult circumstances.

Most of all, as a single, I am reminded that Jesus Christ recognizes me much more than I could ever realize, than I could ever deserve, than I could even know what to do with.

Christ Recognizes You

If He died for you, if God sent His Son to pay the price for your sin, why wouldn't He be concerned about the well-being of your life—about whether you're married or single?

God is concerned. He does love you. He wants to meet your needs right now. He will be with you in your aloneness.

Q. How can you deal with society's reaction to single people?

Q. Should you let other people's remarks or beliefs bother you?

Q. As a single adult, how can you serve God?

Q. Does society pressure you and make you feel you need to marry?

Q. How do you deal with your need to belong?

Q. What role can you play in making a single adult feel less lonely in a church that is couple oriented?

Q. People are not lonely because they are single—many spouses are lonely too. What makes a person lonely?

Q. How can parents work with their children to prevent them from feeling lonely?

Chapter 4

Lonely Spouses

My husband and I have been married for almost two years. We became Christians after being married only six months. There was a dramatic change in both our lives. We were brought out of drugs, and more, by the Lord. But never has my husband given me any of his time. I love him, and I know he loves me, but I don't know how to tell him that I'm terribly lonely. I've asked him to spend time with me, and he lovingly says he'll do better, but he doesn't change.

Before we got married, we used to sit outside and just talk until 3 or 4:00 in the morning. I enjoyed it so much and that's the big reason I married him. I had found a man who liked to talk to me about anything. But as soon as we got married, we never seemed to be alone. He always has friends around.

I have my church family and they are all so special. And we have a little girl now. I thought when we had her I wouldn't be lonely any more. I was wrong. Half of me is missing; even when he's home. I need my mate—the other half of this union.

I have an urge to find a way to avoid writing about the family. Years ago, when my children were young, I made a pact with myself that I would never again speak publicly on the family until they were all grown and I could know if I had been successful with my family life. But now my children are grown and married, and I have grandchildren running around, and I'm still learning.

I take great comfort in the fact that when I was a seminary student, one of my professors told me it isn't necessary to be at the end of the road when you talk about the journey. It is just critical that you be somewhere on the road. I'm not at the end of this road, but I do think I'm making progress toward the goal that God has set before me in His Word.

Every day a part of me struggles with issues related to Christian family life, just as many of you do. If I could say anything at all that would help us all feel better about these challenges, it is that we need to try to be comfortable with the struggle because we're going to have it as long as we live. Even though sometimes we resent anything that upsets the equilibrium of our lives, we need to understand that God wants us to struggle. I don't mean in the bad sense, not in the sense that God purposely causes us suffering and loss to test our faith or to make us grow stronger, but in the sense that He wants us to deal with the biblical truths in our real-life experiences. We always seem to want to do the easy thing, but life is difficult. It takes struggle. Building a good marriage is a part of the struggle.

Marriage is a gift from God, but once He has given us the gift, we need to nurture the marriage and love and care for it. Often we accept the gift and then ignore it, put it on a shelf, so to speak, as if a marriage can survive without further attention. But marriages need time; husbands and wives need attention and affirmation. Without loving care, a marriage relationship stagnates. The result is two lonely people, each searching elsewhere for the joys and fulfillment they should be finding in each other. That is what we'll be thinking about in this chapter.

My strongest comments will be directed at men. That's not because men are lonelier than women, but because many men don't seem to handle the everyday struggles of marriage as well as their wives do. As someone has said, men "don't have the disease [of loneliness], they're carriers." Sometimes it is a matter of mixed-up priorities—a man's overwhelming need to prove his worth in the marketplace and tend to the family with whatever energy, if any, is left over.

I don't know of a better way to demonstrate the way loneliness creeps into a marriage than with the words of some of the people who have written to me describing their marriage experiences. As you read these words, listen to your own heart and consider the needs of your spouse.

Today you really struck a spot that is sensitive. I try not to dwell on it—loneliness in marriage, but the truth is I am lonely. Both my husband and I are Christians. We're both relatively well educated and he is a good man. He works hard and is a good provider. He isn't abusive and he is a fairly good father. But my emotional needs are very rarely met because he is so hard working. It's the case of two people living parallel lives but never really meeting.

He has heard and read a little about how a husband can create a good relationship with his wife, but it must all pass through him without making an impression. I try not to nag. I try not to think about it. But the hurt is deep.

Is there some way I can get across to my husband that I need him—not what he does or earns?

I am an over-the-road trucker. My wife left me several years ago and never came back. I had just gotten saved and had begun to apply biblical principles to our family life, but she thought it was too late.

I remarried last December; and to be honest, I'm scared to death I'll do the same thing with my present wife.

I tried, I really tried, but the pressure of being an over-the-road trucker is awfully hard on a marriage. I spent hours with my ex-wife trying to get her to talk. I asked her what were her needs and how I could meet those needs, but she would never open up.

I get home, and I'm exhausted. I can't seem to move. And then there's the work at the church.

These people think their experiences are unique. Regrettably, however, what they write represents the experience of countless men and women. Perhaps as many as ninety percent of those who get divorced confess that one reason for the breakup of their marriages was the unbearable loneliness of living together but being far apart. The reasons a man neglects his wife and family, the reasons that contribute to loneliness for her, are many leveled. We can't chart them, but a number of things happen as a result, and we can trace those.

Many women respond to the loneliness they feel in their own homes by:

- Getting a job
- Becoming overly involved in church work or community and volunteer organizations
- Joining militant women's groups
- Suffering depression
- Drinking
- Taking tranquilizers
- Using drugs
- Leaving the home

Getting a job and/or becoming involved in church work or community and volunteer organizations are not inappropriate things for a married woman to do unless she does them only to bolster her feelings of self-worth. If she has begun to feel like a non-person and wants to be engaged outside the home solely to have something to point to with pride in order to feel good about herself and there is no other reason, we can feel certain that the basic cause is a non-communicating husband whose attitude toward her implies that her needs are not truly important to him. The men who respond to their wives in this way feel the pattern of everyday life in their homes is set and that they are not going to change. That attitude represents male chauvinism in its truest sense, and it isn't the right way to have a marriage. Shel Silverstein wrote a song called, "Put Another Log on the Fire," that graphically describes a man who uses his wife rather than loves her. While at first reading the sentiments expressed by Silverstein's song may seem a bit heavy handed, actually they aren't. Just substitute some of the everyday demands a man may make on his wife for "go out to the car and change the tire," and so forth, and the real message becomes clear.

Put another log on the fire,
Cook me up some bacon and some beans;
And go out to the car and change the tire,
Wash my socks and sew my old blue jeans.

Come on, Baby, you can fill my pipe,
And then go fetch my slippers,
And boil me up another pot of tea;
Then put another log on the fire, Babe,
And come and tell me why you're
    leavin' me.

Now don't I let you wash the car on Sunday?
Don't I warn you when you're getting fat?
Ain't I gonna take you fishin' someday?
Well, a man can't love a woman more than that.

Ain't I always nice to your kid sister?
Don't I take her drivin' ev'ry night?
So, sit here at my feet,
'Cause I like you when you're sweet,
And you know it ain't feminine to fight.

Come on, Baby, you can fill my pipe,
And then go fetch my slippers,
And boil me up another pot of tea;
Then put another log on the fire, Babe,
And come and tell me why you're leavin' me.[1]

Is it any wonder that a woman whose husband asks her to wait on him as though she were his servant and then tells her she should be grateful for the opportunity to serve, and she should be sweet and not complain, would you feel lonely? Or that she would try to find some way to either make herself feel better or to anesthetize her feelings, at least for a little while? Or that she might become hostile toward men in general because she doesn't know how to deal with one man in particular, the one with whom she should have the most meaningful relationship? Or that she might get fed up with all of it and leave?

These responses to the loneliness of a marriage that is off-track happen throughout our society and the fact that they may be Christians does not make a couple immune, even though we might like to think it does. We like to think that our Christianity will take care of all these matters, but it doesn't.

What I'm talking about may be the best kept secret in the Christian church. You see, when we come to church on Sunday, we come arm in arm. People look at us and say, "My, aren't they a lovely couple. They must have a wonderful life together." Yet in the car before we walked into church, we may have had our worst fight ever. The outer façade is never a very good indication of what's going on inside.

A poem by Edwin Arlington Robinson entitled "Richard Cory," describes the secret loneliness of a man. It shows how carefully we camouflage what's going on inside of us so that others don't know.

> *Whenever Richard Cory went down town*
> *We people on the pavement looked at him:*
> *He was a gentleman from sole to crown,*
> *Clean favored and imperially slim.*
>
> *And he was always quietly arrayed,*
> *And he was always human when he talked;*
> *But still he fluttered pulses when he said,*
> *"Good morning," and he glittered when*
> * he walked.*

And he was rich—yes, richer than a king—
And admirably schooled in every grace;
In fine, we thought that he was everything
To make us wish that we were in his place.

So on we worked, and waited for the light,
And went without the meat, and cursed the bread;
And Richard Cory, one calm summer night,
Went home and put a bullet through his head.[2]

If I've learned anything about people, I've learned that what you see on the outside may not be related to what's going on inside. Some of you reading about this sensitive issue of home relationships are hurting deeply in your hearts, and not even your closest friends know it. You haven't told anyone. Down beneath your façade is a person who cries out because of loneliness. If you are a man who wants to grow in an area that in our culture is a great struggle, then God has something to say to you.

A key verse in Ephesians 5 deals with a husband's responsibility to dispel loneliness in his home. It says:

Husbands, love your wives, just as Christ also loved
the church. (verse 25)

And Paul gives insight into the kind of love that will help us men know how God wants us to meet that responsibility. That love has five characteristics, or principles, that God has given to us describing the relationship of

Christ to the Church as a model of the relationship a husband should have with his wife.

How does Christ love the Church? We men must study it and learn it because it's the way we are to love the woman God has given us as a wife.

• • •

Christ's love is not romantic sentimentalism. Jesus Christ loves the church realistically, and husbands are to love their wives realistically.

One woman said to me, "I never feel that I measure up. No matter what I do, it isn't good enough. So my relationship with my husband is an up and down situation. If I'm good, he loves me. If I'm not, he doesn't." If Christ's love were conditional like that, where would we be? He loves us in spite of who we are, in spite of whether we are "good." That is the most overwhelming aspect of His love for us. He did not love me first, then find out later what I was like and decide if He would continue to love me. He loved me knowing all I would ever do to violate that love. And He keeps right on loving me and you, even to dying on the cross for us.

That's the kind of love that is enjoined on husbands as they relate to their wives. Our love should be, must be, a love that includes faults and failures and all the unlovely and disagreeable elements that are part of human beings. Through Christ, we love in spite of all that. That is the kind of love Christ has for the Church, and it is the kind of love He expects men to have for their wives. One problem many young people face when they marry is that they begin the relationship with unrealistic expectations. Then they discover their marriages aren't what they thought they would be. I think those unrealistic expectations come from watching too much television, from watching too many movies, and from reading too many romantic novels. We even describe the whole process by saying that we "fall in love." You see your love "across a crowded room" during "some enchanted evening," and the next morning you wake up. Reality strikes hard.

This humorous piece exaggerates the expectations, but it also illustrates the principle that reality is far from our romantic ideals:

The Ideal Wife—What Every Man Expects

> *Always beautiful and cheerful.*
> *Could have married movie stars, but wanted only you.*
> *Hair that never needs curlers or beauty shops.*
> *Beauty that won't run in a rainstorm.*
> *Never sick, just allergic to jewelry and fur coats.*
> *Insists that moving the furniture by herself is good for her figure.*
> *Expert in cooking, cleaning house, fixing the car and TV, painting the house, keeping quiet.*
> *Favorite hobbies: mowing the lawn and shoveling snow.*
> *Hates charge plates.*

Her favorite expression is, "What can I do for
  you, dear?"
Thinks you have Einstein's brain but look like
  Mr. America.
Wishes you would go out with the boys so she could
  get some sewing done.
Loves you because you are so good looking.[3]

One of the things I've learned in talking with people whose marriages are hurting is that somehow they've gotten away from love for love's sake and have begun to love for the sake of performance. *One Plus One*, by Tim Timmons, is an excellent book on marriage.[4] It helps you understand what love really is, and it also points to what love isn't. It teaches that your love for your partner is not based on what your partner does for you or on his or her performance. It teaches a simple truth: You love your partner because God has given this person to you to love.

• • •

Christ's love is sacrificial. The Bible says that Jesus Christ counted the cost and gave Himself up for us. His love cost Him His life.

So many people today are trying to find a relationship that doesn't cost anything. They want to receive but are never willing to give. Men love it when somebody preaches on the subject of a wife's "submission" to her husband as found in Ephesians 5:21. But this passage clearly teaches the mutual submission of each one to the other. Love between a man and his wife is a constant giving of one to the other. There is a sense in which a "chain of command" in the home is reflected in Paul's words, but it's also true and present right in this passage that we are to be constantly submitting to each other. Successful marriages occur when mutual submission is a constant ongoing process. They are the blending and giving of ourselves, the determination that we will sacrifice whatever we have to for the sake of our loved ones and our relationships.

The word sacrifice is made up of two Latin words, the first part meaning "holy" and the second part meaning "to make." Sacrifice means we are to make holy at great cost the persons whom we love. This means that if we are going to love our wives as we ought to love them, if that love is going to be the means God uses to dispel the loneliness of their hearts, it will be a love that will cost us time, pleasure, ambition, personal interest, and friends. And it will come to us at this level: Nothing takes priority over my wife, no matter how important anything else may seem. I will love sacrificially.

One woman said that when she asked her husband to spend time with their children or with her, it was always a tentative request. If she became insistent, he said she was nagging.

Honestly, I never wanted anything from him but himself, some part of him, but you can ask for only so long. There is a limit to how long you can be ignored and put off. You threaten to leave, without meaning it, until the day comes when you carry out the threat. You consider all the unpleasant consequences until they don't seem so unpleasant. You decide that nothing could be more unpleasant than being alone and feeling worthless.

Finally you make up your mind that you are going to be a person with real worth as an individual. You assert your ego. You join humankind again. Once again you are a person.

That's what I did. I wanted to be more than a housekeeper, diaper-changer, and sex partner: I wanted to be free from the deep bitterness and guilt that slowly ate at my spiritual and psychological sanity. Deep inside there was something making me not only dislike my husband but dislike everything he did and touched. His "I love you" became meaningless to me because he didn't act like he meant the words. His gifts were evidence to me of his guilt at not spending more time with me. His sexual advances toward me only deepened the gap between us and frustrated us both.

All I wanted was to feel that he really wanted to be with me. But no matter how hard he tried, I always had the feeling I was keeping him from something. Just once I wish he could have canceled something for us instead of cancelling us. All of a sudden one day I woke up and realized I had become a terribly

bitter person. I not only resented my husband and
his work, but I despised myself. So, in desperation,
I left. I don't think he really believed I'd leave him.
But I did.

That's scary. The amazing thing about such a relationship for a man who is totally inattentive to his wife is
that usually he doesn't even suspect what is happening.
In one of his books, Charles Swindoll comments that
"marriages don't ever dissolve because of a blowout; it's
always the result of a slow leak."[5] The breakdown comes
about because of gradual dissipation. At the bottom of
all this lies the fact that someone in the relationship at
some time refused to pay the price to keep the relationship alive.

• • •

Christ loves the church purposefully. He loves the church
in order "that He might present it to Himself a glorious
church, not having spot or wrinkle or any such thing, but
that it should be holy and without blemish" (Ephesians
5:27). The purpose of His love is the development of the
church so that it can be all that He envisions it to be.

The purpose and motivation behind a man's love for
his wife should be that she can become all she should be
as a person. This is opposed to the attitude of the man
who tries to hold back any involvement or growth on the
part of his wife. If he is threatened by any of her gifts or

abilities, he does everything he can to stifle her. He shuts her down as a person until she begins to doubt her own worth.

The Bible teaches that a man who loves his wife will help her develop and mature until she becomes all she should be, all she can be. In God's plan men are facilitators to help make that happen. Someone has adapted a familiar song to say what we're discussing: "Take my wife and let her be consecrated, Lord, to thee." A husband's constant prayer should be, "Lord, just help me to be, in the life of this woman I love, one who encourages her to develop spiritually until she is all that she should be before You." Our desire as husbands should be to love toward that objective.

Christ loves the Church willingly. Does God love us because we are lovable? Absolutely not. He loves us because in His divine prerogative He wills to love us. In times past, in eternity past, God said, "I will love," and He does.

Today the commonly accepted idea about love is: If you don't feel like it, you can't do it. But that's totally counter to the truth. The truth is: Feeling follows action; feeling follows the will. If I want to, I will. When I do, my feelings follow.

Let me give you an illustration. I am a runner. But to be very honest, no matter what all runners say, not one time have I gone out to run because I sincerely wanted to. I never get up in the morning and think, "Wow, isn't it wonderful that today I can begin my morning by running four or five miles!" But when, by an act of will, I get this body going and start to run, the feelings begin to come. It feels most good when I go home, take a shower, relax, and know I've done the right thing. A euphoria exists about it that I can't express.

So let me repeat. The Bible tells us that Christ loves the Church because He wants to, because He wills to. If husbands are to love as Christ loves the Church, we are to love our wives because we want to, because we willingly choose to do the kinds of things our wives regard as loving. We're to perform the actions that go with love. When I was reading the letters to the churches in Revelation recently, something jumped out at me, probably because I was thinking about Christ's love for the Church and how it applies to a husband's love for his wife. The church in Ephesus is told that it has left its first love. Do you recall the prescription for correcting what is wrong? It is: Go back and do the first works (see Revelation 2:1–7).

Let that truth grab hold of you. How do you recover a lost love? Go back to the beginning of the relationship and ask yourself, "What was I doing then that I'm not doing now?" and do it. Take her some flowers. Perhaps you should be sure there's oxygen on hand, but do it. I guarantee she will like it. She'll feel better because you did it, and you'll feel better, too.

If you aren't all the way gone, if it's not too late for you, if there's any hope at all, you'll discover all kinds of things that you feel better for doing. The love that should be in your heart toward the woman who is your wife will begin to develop according to your loving activities. We husbands are responsible to be the leaders in love in our families. That's what it means to be the *head*. We are to be like Christ.

Christ loves the Church absolutely. We are told to love our wives as we love our own bodies (see Ephesians 5:28).

For many years, as I've studied this passage of Scripture and spoken on the subject to couples and young people, I thought this verse meant we are to love our wives just like we love or care about our own bodies. But that's not its full meaning. Paul is telling me that I am to love my wife because she is my body. She is part of me. When you get married, you become one flesh. Just as I will not neglect any part of me that hurts. Together we share unity and oneness.

It's amazing to me how many women hurt deeply and how many husbands don't even suspect. Sometimes a couple is seated in my office to counsel with me about their problems. In a moment of great courage, usually because of the supportive presence of the pastor, the wife blurts out something she's wanted to say for a long time. And the husband will respond, "Why, Honey, I didn't know you felt that way."

I pray every day that God will help me be sensitive to the hurts of my wife, to be able to see when something is wrong that I need to be sensitive to, that I will sense it on her face or in her spirit. Then I can reach out and touch her life as I should. That kind of caring will help dispel the loneliness that so many wives feel.

I am grateful for examples that God has brought into my life to demonstrate the importance of men learning to make family life a priority. One was Jim Dobson. When Jim came to grips with things that were going on in his life, things that were pulling him away from his family, he made some hard decisions. He cut out his speaking engagements. He cut out his traveling. He decided to turn his attention to things he could do at home so he could take care of his family.

I remember one day when I was with Bill Gaither in his office. He was trying to get Jim Dobson to speak at a praise gathering, and he called Jim on the phone while I was there. After the conversation Bill told me, "Jim said he's no longer in the touring-speaking business. He's retired." After that, Bill and Gloria Gaither began to make similar tough decisions about their schedules. They agreed that during two months in the year they would not accept any musical engagements, and Bill totally reorganized his concert schedule in order to be home on certain weekend nights. I said, "Aren't you losing money?" "Yes," he said, "but it's worth it." I looked at the unbelievable pressure of his schedule, and compared it to the meager things God has asked me to do, and thought, "Hey if he can do it, I can." I'm still struggling and sometimes it gets out of hand, and I have to say, "How did this happen to me?" But now I pray I will never lose sight of the biblical priority of my family.

Some of Bill's friends probably think he made a very bad business decision when he canceled those Fridays and Saturdays. But I hope somewhere in eternity they will have the chance to ask him again about priorities!

When we try to love our marriage partner realistically, sacrificially, purposefully, willingly, and absolutely, we begin to come into God's plan; and without thinking of it or planning for it, we find our own needs being met too. Our realistic, sacrificial, purposeful, willing, absolute love comes back to us from our partners, and that is the payoff. Even though Christ has not promised us lives of ease without struggle or pain, He has promised us joy. Husband, love your wife as Christ loved the Church, and count it all joy.

Q. How can you communicate best with your spouse
and prevent his or her feeling alone?

Q. How much time do you and your spouse
spend together?

Q. How can you spend more time with your spouse?

Q. What are the activities you and your spouse
enjoy together?

Q. Are the two of you able to communicate your feelings to each other?

Q. What emotion or feeling can crush loneliness?

Q. What type of love should you have for your spouse?

Q. How can you bring God into your marriage?

Q. According to God's Word, what type of marriage
should you have?

Q. How can you recover lost love?

Chapter 5

Lonely Seniors

I'm just past my eighty-second birthday. I live alone and because of illness I seldom get out to church services. It is not so bad in the summertime when I can be out in my yard for a while each day. But I am really shut in during the winter months.

Sometimes at Christmastime a small group of young people from my church will stop by and sing carols and maybe bring me a gift of fruit. Other than that, though, few visit me or call to offer to help. Would you believe it, I can barely find anyone with time to take me when I have a doctor's appointment.

I prayed for someone to come and help me in my loneliness and thus please the Lord and bring glory to His name. God answered my prayer last winter and sent a dear Christian friend once a week to wash and set my hair and prepare some food that can be kept in the refrigerator for easy serving.

In a rage of anger, a king sentenced a faithful servant to death. Later, regretting what he had done, he summoned the condemned man and said, "In consideration of your long and faithful service to me, I have decided to let you choose the method by which you will die." Without hesitation the servant replied, "I choose to die of old age."

Mentally almost all of us have made the choice to die of old age. But, even though we have decided we want to grow old, we don't deal with the aging process very well. Instead we get caught up in a multifaceted quest for the fountain of youth. One wag put it this way:

> *Between the two choices of life*
> *What a spread—*
> *To stop getting older*
> *You have to be dead!*

Sooner or later we become preoccupied with aging. Geriatrics is flourishing. This specialized branch of research investigates the infirmities and maladies of the elderly and seeks to find remedies. Yet in spite of countless stimulants, hormones, pep pills, and longevity programs, people still grow old, and mostly we resent the process.

Although we haven't learned much about aging gracefully and comfortably, we have managed to prolong life. At the turn of the twentieth century, when the average life expectancy was forty-seven years, there were 4.9

million Americans over sixty. That number rose drastically in the early 90s, when the average life expectancy was seventy-five years, totaling more than 30 million Americans over the age of sixty-five.[1] As of 2009, 40 million people in the United States were sixty-five and older with a life expectancy of eighty-three years.

Because of improved health care and other medical advances, the elderly now comprise a larger percentage of the population than ever before. In fact, since 1900 the number of people sixty years old and older has increased four times faster than those who are under sixty and the trend toward a larger elderly population will continue. In 2010, there were twenty-two people aged sixty-five and older to every 100 people of traditional working age (20 to 64). By 2050, these older Americans are predicted to represent twenty percent of the entire population, totaling 88.5 million people.[2] Between 2008 and 2009, health specialists calculated a 3.4 percent decrease in the mortality rate of sixty-five to seventy-four year olds and a 4.9 percent decrease in seventy-five to eighty-four year olds.[3]

These are wonderful advances for mankind but, in spite of medical progress, older people are among our loneliest citizens. Each year the number of their friends diminishes. Their lifetime companions die and they are alone. They miss the fellowship of their contemporaries and loved ones. As their vigor abates, their world contracts, and little by little their sense of self-worth and importance shrinks. They begin to feel useless.

As our population gets grayer, the problems of aging

become more apparent—not necessarily more acute, but certainly more noticeable. Because some of the elderly have tried to cope by organizing, senior citizens groups have grown up all over the country. For example, the National Council of Senior Citizens has three million members, and the American Association of Retired Persons boasts a membership of more than nine million. The Gray Panthers, led by Maggie Kuhn, a spry woman in her seventies, has a team of lawyers that investigates retirement and nursing homes, and lobbies Congress for better legislation to protect the elderly. All these groups have the objective of improving the lifestyle and base of support for the elderly.

It is the loss of a sense of control and independence that is the most frightening to anticipate—the vulnerability and the helplessness that come with declining health and a greater need for assistance. It seems that the "golden years" lose their glow and many elderly wonder what is left to live for. Maggie Kuhn feels this is due at least in part to society's perception of when one becomes old and what being old actually means. The sudden loss of a reason to get up in the morning can be devastating to those who have always, throughout their lives, had a reason. Kuhn says, "Fixed retirement is dehumanizing. It shows how stupid our society is in making scrap piles of the elderly."[4] When the feeling of usefulness declines, fairly quickly health problems take on a greater importance than anything else. But, according to Kuhn, that is often a result of life situations. "Much of senility is not irreversible," says Kuhn. "It is induced by despair and frustration."[5]

Christians ought to know more about aging. The loneliness we face as we grow older seems to grip us with the same tenacity as it does those who are not Christian. Christianity does not make us immune to the pain of aloneness when we lose a mate or a close friend, or guarantee we will deal well with a growing feeling of unimportance. We Christians don't seem to reflect the creative difference that growing older "in Christ" ought to make. Someone has said, "The devil has no happy old people." It seems the Lord doesn't have many either. More often than not, we hear older people say, "I really don't know why I'm still alive and in this world. What is there for me to do? What is the purpose of my existence now?"

An elderly woman who lived alone in a one-room apartment was found dead. The medical examiner determined she had been dead for a week, perhaps as long as two weeks. Her diary lay open on the stand beside the chair in which she died. The daily entries for the last months of her life said, "Nobody came to see me today." The very last one, however, was different. It said, "Still nobody came to see me today." To die alone is one thing; to die in loneliness is a tragedy.

How should we deal with the loneliness of old age? Those of us who are able can visit and offer to help. Just think of the blessing the Christian friend described in the letter at the beginning of this chapter brought in the form of a little cooking and other assistance during her weekly visits. Another of my correspondents suggests we begin early to teach our youth to interact with those among us who need attention and assistance. She says,

> Severe loneliness can bring on illness and sometimes death. Why hasn't the body of Christ recognized the seriousness of this? Why not train young people to visit and help widows and orphans, the isolated poor, the friendless?

Do you remember what Christ said about helping others?

> Inasmuch as you did it to one of the least of these My brethren, you did it to Me.
>
> (Matthew 25:40)

I'm not talking about forcing our help on those who don't want it for the sake of making ourselves feel good, but finding those who need assistance of some kind and giving of ourselves for their sakes in a spirit of Christlikeness.

We should plan to do what we can all our lives to give of ourselves, no matter what age we happen to be, no matter what changes take place in our lives.

> My husband went to be with the Lord several years ago. I can identify with the problems of loneliness, but the Lord is very precious. There is a dimension to my life that I never had before. Many people confide

their problems in me and ask me to pray for them. I teach Sunday school and am involved in other church activities.

To be open to others, to listen, to pray with them and for them—that is something vital we can do at any age.

I've been looking around in my Christian world for examples of men and women who are growing older with the outlook I anticipated Christians should have. Then I began to look through the Scriptures to see if I could discover a biblical model of someone who grew old well. One stands out: Caleb, a man from the tribe of Judah, the son of Jephunneh.

Caleb first appears in the book of Numbers as one of Judah's representatives in the foray into Kadesh-Barnea (see Numbers 13:6). He and his friend Joshua brought back the minority report. It was bad news—Caleb was almost stoned by his hearers. But there was also good news—Caleb and Joshua were the only two contemporary adults who were allowed to live long enough to see the Promised Land. As we begin to look at his story, Caleb was eighty-five years old and about to experience the greatest moment in his life.

Caleb's experience illustrates two important truths guaranteed to dispel loneliness in our senior years: what we consider "old age," and it is never time to retire from the Lord's work.

I see three principles emerge from Caleb's life that provide a path away from old age loneliness.

Keep growing physically

> The Lord has kept me alive, as He said, these forty-five
> years, ever since the Lord spoke this word to Moses
> while Israel wandered in the wilderness; and now,
> here I am this day, eighty-five years old. As yet I am as
> strong this day as on the day that Moses sent me; just
> as my strength was then, so now is my strength for
> war, both for going out and for coming in.
>
> (Joshua 14:10–11)

Caleb was as strong at eighty-five as he had been at forty. A similar statement was made of Moses when he was 120: "His eye was not dim, nor his natural force abated" (Deuteronomy 34:7 KJV).

Most of the time, we downplay the importance of the physical. The "outer man" hasn't received the attention he (or she) deserves. We become so concerned with our spirituality, we forget that the spiritual part of us needs a body in which to walk around. C. S. Lewis pointed to the critical relationship between soul and body when he wrote: "Our body and souls live so close together that they catch each other's diseases."[6]

Many of us work hard at ignoring the frustrations of growing older, and one of the methods we employ is senior citizen humor. For example, a little girl was sitting on her grandfather's lap. She looked at his white hair and wrinkled skin and asked, "Grandpa, did God make you?" Yes, Honey. He surely did," he answered. Looking at herself and examining her smooth skin, she asked, "And did God make me?" "Yes, God made you too," was the reply. The little girl thought for a few seconds and then said, "Don't you think God's doing a better job than He used to?"

Another little girl asked her dad if he was on the ark with Noah. When he said absolutely not, she wanted to know why he hadn't drowned.

Because it is innocent, children's humor related to old age isn't so hard to take. But I'm not sure that other ways of poking fun at the elderly are as palatable. For instance, have you heard these quips?

You know you're growing old when . . .
   . . . most everything hurts, and what doesn't hurt, doesn't work.
   . . . you get winded playing chess.
   . . . you join a health club and don't go.
   . . . you sink your teeth into a steak and they stay there.
   . . . the little gray-haired lady you help across the street is your wife.
   . . . you bend down to pick up something and you ask yourself, "Is there anything else I should do while I'm down here?"

And I'm sure you've heard this folk song:

   How do I know my youth is all spent?
   My get-up-and-go has got up and went.

My joints are stiff and filled with pain.
The pills that I take, they give me no gain.
I rub in the ointment, like fury I do.
Each pain when it leaves, comes back with two.
But in spite of it all, I am able to grin,
When I think of the places my get-up has been.

Old age is golden I have heard it said.
But sometimes I wonder as I get into bed,
My ears on the dresser, my teeth in a cup,
My eyes on the table till I wake up.
E're sleep comes each night, I say to myself,
"Is there anything else I should lay on the shelf?"[7]

It's all right to laugh at ourselves, but let's not use humor as a smoke screen to cover neglect and abuse of our bodies.

A resident of a retirement village showed me around her apartment and then showed me where she exercises. That particular village is large with long hallways. I think you easily could run a 10,000-meter race in there. This woman and a friend meet at a certain time each morning, and they walk the halls of that place, up and down, from one end to the other, just as fast as they can walk.

Right on! That's what God intends us to do. These bodies of ours ought not to be allowed to deteriorate just because we're getting older. Most of all we need to keep our attitudes healthy. That is the best way to keep our bodies healthy.

It seems that most men and women begin to give up on themselves at about age forty. Perceptions of health are fairly well established by that age and tend to set the tone for the rest of our lives. But Caleb was able to do at eighty-five what he did at forty even though he had good reason to allow himself to decline.

Think of it. When he was at the prime of his life, what was his assignment? The desert. That's right, he could look forward to spending forty years in the desert with nothing much more exciting to do than bury the dead who had chosen not to believe God. And while Caleb was engaged in that discouraging activity, Moses died, and Joshua was chosen to replace him. Caleb was passed over. Many men would have given up on life right then and stopped caring about themselves. But Caleb didn't do that, and when God was ready for him, Caleb was prepared to walk on stage and play his part in the drama of Israel's relocation.

John Wesley was a Caleb-type. At eighty-five he said he was not weary with travel or preaching, and you'd think that if anyone might get tired, he would. He had traveled over 250,000 miles on horseback, had preached over 40,000 sermons, and had written 400 books while learning and speaking ten languages. Wesley attributed his vigor at eighty-five to four things:

1. Exercise and change of air
2. Never having lost a night's sleep on land or sea

3. Rising at 4:00 every morning
4. Preaching at 5:00 each morning for fifty years

When Wesley was eighty-six, he was annoyed that he couldn't write for more than fifteen hours a day. At eighty-seven he was ashamed that he couldn't preach more than twice a day, and he confessed to a growing urge to lie in bed after 5:30 in the morning.

Our bodies are temples of the Holy Spirit, and there is no reason to believe we should stop caring for the temple after it reaches a certain age. So, keep your body strong. If you can't run, walk. If you can't walk, shuffle. But don't give up on yourself physically.

Keep growing mentally

> Now therefore, give me this mountain of which the Lord spoke in that day; for you heard in that day how the Anakim were there, and that the cities were great and fortified. It may be that the Lord will be with me, and I shall be able to drive them out as the Lord said.
>
> (Joshua 14:12)

So many people stop dreaming. Their senior years are spent in loneliness and boredom because they've lost their dreams.

Since I have retired from life's competition,
Each day is filled with complete repetition.

I get up every morning and dust off my wits,
Go pick up the paper and read the o'bits.
If my name isn't there, I know I'm not dead.
I eat a good breakfast and go back to bed.[8]

Caleb wasn't like that. He was by far the oldest, yet he asked for the toughest assignment. His contemporaries were dead and buried in the desert. The other men who were assigned an inheritance to claim were younger, but they weren't getting the job done. And Joshua was old, his days about gone, and the thing God had instructed him to do wasn't getting done: "Now Joshua was old, advanced in years. And the Lord said to him: 'You are old, advanced in years, and there remains very much land yet to be possessed'" (Joshua 13:1).

In addition, we have clearly preserved for us the fact of the young Israelites' failure to do what God had commanded: "There remained among the children of Israel seven tribes which had not yet received their inheritance. Then Joshua said to the children of Israel: 'How long will you neglect to go and possess the land which the Lord God of your fathers has given you?'" (Joshua 18:2–3)

But what they had failed to do, eighty-five-year-old Caleb did. He was a tough-minded man in a weak-minded generation. He continued to be mentally what he had been at forty in Kadesh-Barnea. He teaches us that it is the attitudes of our hearts not our activities or ages that determine whether we are young or old.

Old age did not dim the enthusiasm of great leaders

of the past. I've already told you about John Wesley, but there were others such as John Knox, who at eighty-four was said to preach with as much power as ever; Benjamin Franklin, who served his country most effectively when he was past sixty and was U.S. Ambassador to France when he was in his eighties; Gladstone, who led England when he was eighty-three; and Bismarck, who vigorously administered the affairs of state for the German Empire when he was seventy-four.

The truth is, you are old at forty if you have stopped accepting challenges. If we think of the future only in terms of security, we have already set the stage for a lonely and discouraging old age lifestyle. In *There's a Lot More to Health Than Not Being Sick*, Bruce Larson says:

> A life of safety is no life at all, whatever your vocation. Still, we are programmed from an early age to start providing for a safe and secure future. Through pension funds and retirement benefits, we work toward removing all risk from our lives by the time we are 65. Yet in the three societies sociologists have studied where people normally live to 100 and frequently to 120, there is no special treatment for the aged. There are no retirement homes where people can spend their declining years playing shuffleboard. Scientists who had studied these societies have found they have nothing in common in terms of climate, diet, geography or lifestyle. But in all three places, the inhabitants

are expected to live normal lives with no cushion for safety. They continue to work, tend fields and keep shops until they die at 100 plus.

I am convinced that God never invented old age. Death is a gift, but old age is man's invention. It is a cultural blight in our lifetime.[9]

Caleb never stopped dreaming and growing, and God used him until his dying day.

Keep growing spiritually

Nevertheless my brethren who went up with me made the heart of the people melt, but I wholly followed the Lord my God.

(Joshua 14:8)

Of Caleb, God said, "But My servant Caleb, because he has a different spirit in him and has followed Me fully, I will bring into the land where he went, and his descendants shall inherit it" (Numbers 14:24).

Moses also testified to Caleb's faithfulness: "So Moses swore on that day, saying, 'Surely the land where your foot has trodden shall be your inheritance and your children's forever, because you [Caleb] have wholly followed the Lord my God'" (Joshua 14:9). Caleb subdued and drove out his enemies, giants and all, because he wholly followed the Lord. He entertained no divided loyalties. He remembered God's promises. Three times in Joshua

14, the record shows Caleb referring to what the Lord said about him. Those promises kept Caleb going during many years. He started believing God early in life and never stopped growing spiritually.

Remember the Kadesh-Barnea days? The majority report came back from Canaan, a report filled with giants, strong people, great walled villages, and ultimate defeat. But Caleb refused to give in to pessimism and defeatism. He saw Canaan, not as an obstacle, but as an opportunity.

> Caleb quieted the people . . . and said, "Let us go up at once and take possession, for we are well able to overcome . . . The land . . . is an exceedingly good land . . . which flows with milk and honey . . .
>
> Only do not . . . fear the people of the land, for they are our bread; their protection has departed from them, and the Lord is with us. Do not fear them."
>
> (Numbers 13:30; 14:7–9)

That positive spirit kept him strong. He was a brave man among cowards, an assured man among skeptics. As his age changed, his attitude soared above his circumstances. Ours can too.

Sherwood Eliot Wirt has written a book entitled *I Don't Know What Old Is, But Old Is Older Than Me.*[7] Wirt talks about travel, reading, music, and spending the retirement years doing some of those things there wasn't time for because earning a living and rearing a family were all consuming. He mentions the need for those who are struggling through their own and seemingly unique experiences. Underlying all of Wirt's book, however, is the message that at any time of life, no matter our ages or our circumstances, God has something for each of us to do. We need to find out what that is and do it. When we do that, we dispel loneliness not only in our own lives but also in the lives of those we touch. And we can begin to have the right attitude about aging.

I'm sure that's what Solomon meant in the book of Proverbs when he wrote that the beauty of old age is the gray head, and the "silver-haired head is a crown of glory, if it is found in the way of righteousness" (Proverbs 16:31).

John E. Roberts expressed sentiments about aging that really do put the whole matter into perspective. I think he points our attention to one of the greatest promises of all.

> They say that I am growing old,
> I've heard them tell it times untold,
> In language plain and bold—
> But I'm not growing old.
> This frail old shell in which I dwell
> Is growing old, I know full well—
> But I am not the shell.
>
> What if my hair is turning gray?
> Gray hairs are honorable, they say.

What if my eyesight's growing dim?
I still can see to follow Him
Who sacrificed His life for me
Upon the Cross of Calvary.

What should I care if Time's old plough
Has left its furrows on my brow?
Another house, not made with hand,
Awaits me in the Glory Land.

What though I falter in my walk?
What though my tongue refuse to talk?
I still can tread the Narrow Way,
I still can watch, and praise and pray.

My hearing may not be as keen
As in the past it may have been,
Still I can hear my Saviour say
In whispers soft, "This is the way."

The outward man, do what I can
To lengthen out this life's short span,
Shall perish, and return to dust,
As everything in nature must.
The inward man, the scriptures say,
Is growing stronger every day.

Then how can I be growing old
When safe within my Saviour's fold?

E're long my soul shall fly away,
And leave this tenement of clay,
This robe of flesh I'll drop and rise
To seize the "everlasting prize."
I'll meet you on the Streets of Gold,
And prove that I'm not growing old.[10]

Q. How can you help a senior stop feeling lonely or, as a senior citizen, what can you do to stop feeling lonely?

Q. How can you help a senior citizen improve his or her sense of self-worth?

Q. Why should Christians learn more about aging?

Q. How can we use Caleb as an example to follow?

Q. How does our physical shape affect our mental and physical mindsets?

Q. How can we use John Wesley as an example?

Q. What do John Wesley and Caleb have in common? How do they differ?

Q. How can we remain strong?

Chapter 6

Lonely Servants

Those eighteen years in the ministry made me look and feel ten years older than I was. I spent them holding people's hands, smoothing out countless interpersonal battles and church struggles, preaching how many hundreds of sermons, baptizing people. Marrying them, burying them. As the church grew, so did the traffic to my office. I was not surprised at that, nor was I unaware of my calling and the demands I had to face in serving. But in all that time I could not find a confidant, someone who could simply listen and pray with me, not even my wife understood my need for that. Those burdens were heavy.

While I struggled to find new and fresh sermon material, time for my own relaxed devotional life disappeared. When the church reached 1,200 members from the first 300, it was a sign of great blessing from God on my work. I accepted that and thanked Him for it. But at the same time, I found myself even more lonely as the demands on my time tripled. My family was growing up and away from me. When I saw my children graduate from high school and then college, I realized I hardly knew them. I knew then I had to do something, although I was a little late.

I concluded I could not abide that lonely road any longer. I knew I had to find some area of work where I could establish normal human relationships. Maybe I'm just was not cut out to be a leader after all.

All servants of God with a heart for people sometimes experience the loneliness that comes in attempting to carry the burdens of others. More than once, they will be tempted to cry out as Moses did, "I cannot carry all these people by myself; the burden is too heavy for me" (Numbers 11:14 NIV). No man or woman can be prepared for that experience of aloneness. Each of us has to learn the hard way.

In order to lead, the leader must walk ahead of the group, and that separates him or her from the followers. There is a sense then in which leading means turning your back on the very ones you are trying to serve with leadership. In promoting their interests, articulating their values, helping them to define their goals, the leader loses his freedom. But leaders need to fulfill their own potential and not be absorbed completely by the group's needs. Attempting to fill that kind of role often causes troubling loneliness. A missionary describes the loneliness as an everyday burden:

You feel alone in the task, realizing that there are no times of applause from anyone, no fitting into the social whirl of the good life at home, never really being a part of people in the normal concourses of life, because a missionary is, after all, a breed apart. That is the crushing load of the cross for me.

Another missionary says:

The worst part of it is that in twenty years of missions' service I have never gotten close enough to anyone at home to really call them a friend. People pray for me, as they said, when my name comes up on the church's prayer calendar, but they can't pray for me as somebody they really know. On home leave, I never confess a human weakness. Nobody wants to listen to that. It is embarrassing to them. Everyone assumes a life of faith has no human frailties. To admit to them would destroy the people's ideal image that God dominates human chemistry. So they keep me above all that; they can't allow me to come down to where they are. I have to be on some level above them in order for them to maintain their trust in me as their missionary.

Home leave is often a time of tears for me; it always has been. I desperately want people to accept me into their inner circle as a person and not think of me as a superhuman frontier warrior. I want to cry with them, laugh with them. I want them to do the same with me. Instead, we meet, we talk, we pass each other. I do my act, they applaud, and that is that.

The New Testament provides insight into the loneliness of leadership. In Paul's letters we have the opportunity to look into his life and view his solitude. His pastoral letters to Timothy and Titus are especially helpful for, as Demetrius said, "Everyone reveals his soul in his letters."[1] These epistles show us the heart of the aging apostle.

Paul's second letter to Timothy is perhaps his most personal communication. When writing to his young friend who was pastoring in Ephesus, Paul was open about the loneliness he was experiencing.

The Loneliness of Danger

Paul was in prison in Rome. Outside in the streets, Nero's persecution was in full swing. Behind the façade of sophisticated Roman society lay total moral decay and a growing disregard for human life. Suicide was rampant: Men and women, tired of the struggle, gave up and put an end to themselves. Following the fire of A.D. 63, that had burned half of Rome, Nero, who was responsible for it, had successfully blamed his crime on the Christians.

Many of those Christians were Paul's personal friends. Huddled in his cold cell, Paul died inwardly as the fate of Christian brothers and sisters was revealed. Some of them had been covered with the skins of beasts and thrown to wild animals. Some burned as human torches while Nero drove his chariot around the gardens, indulging his warped mind in a carnival of fire and blood. Danger, terror, and persecution were in the air. Paul, isolated in his prison room, could do nothing but grieve for his friends and anticipate an equally horrible end to his own life.

The Loneliness of Despair

Off and on throughout his ministry, Paul had known the trauma of imprisonment. Most scholars believe his last confinement was in the infamous Mamertine Prison. If they are correct, his cell was damp and reeked with pestilence, reminding him of the miseries of generations of condemned criminals. No wonder he asked for his coat (see 2 Timothy 4:13).

Paul knew he would not escape from that cell alive. He had had his preliminary audience with Caesar, and although he had not been condemned to die then (see 2 Timothy 4:16–17), it was just a matter of time. Public feeling toward the apostle and his converts was hostile. Most people viewed allegiance to the Lord Jesus Christ as high treason. The dark cloud that hung over Paul is apparent in his words of resignation: "For I am now ready to be offered, and the time of my departure is at hand. I have fought a good fight, I have finished my course, I have kept the faith" (2 Timothy 4:6–7 KJV).

Tradition has it that Paul was condemned to death and then beheaded as a Roman citizen on the Ostian Way about three miles outside the city. According to Christian historian Eusebius, Peter was executed on the same day by upside-down crucifixion. Though we cannot validate the actual details of either death, we do know that Paul's second letter to Timothy was his last will and testament to the church. Shivering in his prison cell, he was writing with the knowledge that he would not write again.

The Loneliness of Detachment and Defection

Paul's greatest pain was not the deprivation of his Roman cell, but his separation from his caring companions. His anguish is clear when he speaks to Timothy about rejection and reveals that all who were in Asia had turned against him, including Phygellus and Hermogenes (see 2 Timothy 1:15). Demas had forsaken him; Crescens had gone to Galatia and Titus to Dalmatia (4:10). Paul had sent Tychicus to Ephesus (4:12). Alexander, the coppersmith, had been on a rampage (4:14). Erastus had been left back in Corinth, and Trophimus was sick at Miletus (4:20). Seemingly almost all of Paul's friends had evaporated at the time of his preliminary hearing before Caesar (see 4:16–17). We feel the pain of his loneliness in the words, "Only Luke is with me" (4:11).

Bishop Handley Moule reminds us of Paul's vulnerability and human frailty:

I have often found it difficult to deliberately read these short chapters without finding something like a mist gathering in my eyes. The writer's heart beats in the writing. You can see his tears fall over the dear past and the harrowing present. Yet in spite of all of this, there is a noble solemnity. Here is a man on his way to death, and that he must say his words now or never, suffuses the whole composition. One moment he is strong with courage and the next he is tender as a child, when he begs his friend Timothy to come to him before winter, because he is so lonely.

From his majestic survey of the past ("I have fought the good fight") and his confident anticipation of the future ("Henceforth there is laid up for me the crown"), Paul returns in thought to the present and to his own personal predicament. For the great apostle Paul was also a creature of flesh and blood, a man of like nature and passions with ourselves. Although he has finished his course and is awaiting his crown, he is still a frail human being with ordinary human needs. He describes his plight in prison, and expresses in particular his loneliness.[2]

Demas' desertion was obviously painful to Paul. Previously he had been one of Paul's close associates, a "fellow worker." In the other two New Testament verses that mention Demas, his name is coupled with Luke's (see Colossians 4:14 and Philemon 24). But now, instead of loving Christ's appearance as Paul did (see 2 Timothy 4:10), Demas had embraced the present world system. The details of his defection are not divulged, but the reign of terror under which he was living may have frightened him.

A leader knows the biting hurt that comes when someone in whom he has invested much time turns away from the faith, and sometimes turns against the leader as well. I remember how I felt when a family I had personally won to Christ turned against me because of things said by a disloyal staff member. I don't remember, before or since in my life, experiencing hurt like that.

Paul wrote in particular about the fierce opposition of a man named Alexander. This is probably a different Alexander from "Alexander the heretic" (see 1 Timothy 1:20) or "Alexander the orator" (see Acts 19:33). The phrase describing his deeds might be translated: "He informed many evil things against me." Some writers believe that Alexander was the informer responsible for Paul's second arrest. What Paul says here, however, is that he "strongly opposed our message" (2 Timothy 4:14–15 NIV).

Thinking back over my ministerial career, I find my heart encouraged by the knowledge of the opposition to

Paul. That kind of difficulty has triggered loneliness in me, too. (Paul's willingness to let the Lord reward the deeds of his opponents is a lesson I am still struggling to learn.) No leader who determines to walk the high road with his God will be able to escape that experience. I am comforted at such times by the words spoken by John about Christ: "He was in the world, and the world was made by Him, and the world knew him not. He came unto His own, and His own received him not" (John 1:10–11 KJV).

Dr. A. B. Simpson described his ministerial loneliness by saying he often was so misunderstood that he would look down at the paving stones in the street for the sympathy denied him elsewhere. Yet at the same time he knew God was preparing him and molding him for a ministry of distinction in the future. Founder of the Christian and Missionary Alliance denomination, Simpson left behind five schools for the training of missionaries, hundreds of missionaries in sixteen lands, and a large number of congregations in the United States and Canada that over the years have exerted a spiritual influence far beyond their numerical strength. Often the crowd does not recognize a leader until he is gone, and then they build a monument for him with the stones they threw at him in life.[3]

When Paul wrote in 2 Timothy about his first defense before Caesar, he was referring to the preliminary hearing that under Roman law preceded the formal trial. According to law, Paul had the right to call a lawyer or witnesses. But not one of the Christians in Rome would speak in his defense. "No one stood with me," he said (4:16).

As Paul was called before Caesar, accused of disloyalty to the state and "atheism"—which to the Romans meant the refusal of idolatry or emperor worship—he was alone. This was his Gethsemane. It could now be said of him as it was of his Lord, "They all forsook him and fled" (Mark 14:50).

Yet in spite of difficulties and desertion by others, Paul also gives us insight into some of the encouragement we can feel during such hours.

Physical Encouragement

The part of Paul's loneliness that related to his body cannot be disregarded. His cloak, left with Carpus in Troas (see 2 Timothy 4:13), was an outer garment corresponding to an overcoat. Such cloaks in Paul's day were needed during the very cold winter months, and winter was coming (v. 21).

Several commentators point out the historical parallel between Paul's imprisonment in Rome and William Tyndale's in Belgium nearly fifteen centuries later.

In 1535, immured by the persecutor at Vilvoorde in Belgium, [Tyndale] wrote not long before his fiery martyrdom, a Latin letter to the Marquis of Bergen, governor of the castle: "I entreat your lordship, and that by the Lord Jesus, that if I must remain here for the winter you would beg the commissary to be so kind as to send me, from the things of mine which he has, a warmer cap; I feel the cold painfully in my head. Also a warmer cloak, for the cloak I have is very thin. He has a woolen shirt of mine if he will send it. But most of all, my Hebrew Bible, grammar and vocabulary, that I may spend my time in that pursuit."[4]

Personal Encouragement

Our most obvious need in time of loneliness is companionship. The Lord is always with us, but most of us are like the little boy who was told that he shouldn't be afraid of the dark because the Lord was with him. "I know that," he replied, "but I want somebody with skin on." Paul was not different from us. He encouraged Timothy to bring Mark with him—the same Mark who had once deserted Paul but had now been restored. Paul missed him and wanted to see him once more.

Most of all, Paul wanted to be with Timothy again. "Do your best to come to me quickly" (2 Timothy 4:9 NIV). "Do your best to get here before winter" (verse 21 NIV). Paul seemed to know he would not survive the winter. He also knew that once winter came, Timothy would not be able to get through to Rome. It shouldn't be difficult for us to reconcile Paul's longing to be with Christ and his longing to see Timothy again. Both longings lie within the heart of the leader/servant.

Mental Encouragement

Paul mentioned to Timothy his desire for "the books, especially the parchments" (4:13). The difference between the two was probably that the books were made of papyrus. Those papyrus rolls could have included any number of things, perhaps Paul's Roman citizenship papers, correspondence, or extra writing materials. The parchments may have been Paul's copies of the Old Testament Scriptures in Greek or the collected words of Jesus Christ. Paul wanted to use his isolated hours redemptively. Studying what he accomplished during his terms in prison ought to make us all reevaluate our activity-packed schedules.

The loneliness of servanthood can often be a means to direct us into times of protracted study and meditation. Driven to this sometimes by my own loneliness, I have found great relief. The greatest challenge is to get over the initial emotional hurdle. At such times one doesn't feel like studying, reading, or meditating. But I find that when I take the step of faith to do what I know I should do, my feelings begin to change. I am buoyed up. My heart is encouraged.

Spiritual Encouragement

When Paul stood alone before Caesar, he was not really alone. "The Lord stood with me" (4:17). When it is possible for us to minister to lonely servants in some tangible way, we should never excuse ourselves by saying, "Well, the Lord will be with them." On the other hand, the Lord's presence is anyone's greatest hope for lasting help. Paul said, "The Lord will deliver me . . . and preserve me" (v. 18).

As I am finishing this chapter, the Lord is allowing me to experience a time of intense loneliness. And I have been reminded of some great promises in the books of Isaiah. They jump across the centuries to lift my spirit.

> Have you not known?
> Have you not heard?
> The everlasting God, the Lord,
> The Creator of the ends of the earth,
> Neither faints nor is weary.
> His understanding is unsearchable.
> He gives power to the weak,
> And to those who have no might He increases strength.
> Even the youths shall faint and be weary,
> And the young men shall utterly fall,
> But those who wait on the Lord
> Shall renew their strength;
> They shall mount up with wings like eagles,

They shall run and not be weary,
They shall walk and not faint.

(Isaiah 40:28–31)

Fear not, for I am with you;
Be not dismayed, for I am your God.
I will strengthen you,
Yes, I will help you,
I will uphold you with My righteous right hand.

(Isaiah 41:10)

But now, thus says the Lord, who created you, O Jacob,
And He who formed you, O Israel:
"Fear not, for I have redeemed you;
I have called you by name;
You are Mine.
When you pass through the waters, I will be with you;
And through the rivers, they shall not overflow you.
When you walk through the fire, you shall not be
*   burned,*
Nor shall the flame scorch you.
For I am the Lord your God,
The Holy One of Israel, your Savior."

(Isaiah 43:1–3)

Q. What do servants need to ease their loneliness?

Q. Who should servants remember is always with them?

Q. What can you do to help your leaders?

Q. What lessons should we learn from Paul?

Q. How can faith relate to loneliness?

Q. How can danger, despair, and detachment relate to loneliness? How can they be overcome?

Q. Explain the statement: "To lead is to turn one's back on people."

Q. How can servants be lonely?

Q. How can you make servants in your community feel less lonely?

Q. How would you describe leadership loneliness?

Chapter 7

Lonely Sufferers

It was when the lights went out and the room was suddenly plunged into darkness that the awful awareness came. The traffic of the hospital went on like an uncontrolled fever outside my door. But inside that room it became still, so still that you could sense, even believe, that the walls were moving and the room was becoming smaller.

I was never a lonely person up until then. At least, I don't recall being lonely. But now I knew what it was. My family had gone home together to that familiar, safe place. But I was here alone, isolated, facing the uncertainties of what hospitals mean.

Up to that moment I had joked and laughed with friends and family because it all seemed like a lark. But now I knew. Suddenly I swallowed hard against the pressure in my chest. I was a little girl again, wanting someone to put on a light somewhere to cut the darkness, so I could get to sleep. I became terrified by the feeling. Sleep was a long time coming—hours of trying to push my mind off the emptiness, fear, and darkness. The hospital slowly grew quiet, almost eerie, until there was only silence.[1]

A close reading of Psalm 116 reveals that David, the psalmist, had an experience with serious illness. He vividly describes the human characteristics of suffering: the despair, the fear, the terror, the sense of a loss of control over life, the loneliness, and the feelings of abandonment. In part he says:

> *The pains of death encompassed me,*
> *And the pangs of Sheol [Hell] laid hold of me;*
> *I found trouble and sorrow.*(v.3)

In sickness there is physical pain to be dealt with, but the pain of despair and fear of an unknown outcome must be borne in the intimacy of your own person. Despair becomes depression. The anguish of suffering causes tears to come. You feel as if you're losing your equilibrium emotionally and physically.

A forty-three-year-old man, taken to the hospital fearing he had cancer, described in present-day language what David talks about in Psalm 116.

> Everything about me was on a chart. I wasn't a name, except when they had to remind themselves who I was by checking my wristband. All of my body chemistry was on that chart. They knew what my blood was like, what pills I took and when, what my elimination

habits were—they even knew through a monitoring system how I breathed, how my heart reacted to every move.

All of what was supposed to be me was on a sheaf of papers, but no one bothered to know me really. Here I was, a gregarious person who liked to laugh, and who cared. No one asked what made me cry, or if I liked to fish or go boating, or what sports I enjoyed, what food I liked to eat—none of that was relevant. I was not a human being, but an object of sticking and probing and testing and experimenting with. They stood over me and hummed or grunted or sighed or whispered off to one side. Seldom did anybody tell me what they were discussing. It all went on my chart, but none of it into my ears.

I was left to my own imagination of what was wrong—how serious it was—whether it meant a life of inactivity with my job on the line, becoming a burden to my family. After a while I sank deeper into the doldrums. I thought I was strong enough to lick anything that happened to me. But lying there day after day with my fears playing havoc with my mind and emotions, I was reduced to being a child.

One night I let the tears come. That was a shock, to realize I had come to a place of such total helplessness and despair and anxiety.[2]

David also feared he would become dependent, that his feet would fall (v.8). He said, "I believed, therefore I spoke, 'I am greatly afflicted'" (v.10). I suppose for men that's one of the most difficult parts of being sick. We think of ourselves as self-sufficient and independent and responsible for others, and suddenly we find ourselves in the hospital. At first it may seem kind of neat to be there, having someone caring for you like that. But fairly soon you wish they would just go away. You don't want to see anyone who's coming to help; you want to do it yourself.

Someone has said that we spend our lives learning how to clothe ourselves sensibly, modestly, fashionably, and attractively. Then we go to the hospital, and it all unravels with the indignity of that horrible invention, the "hospital gown." No matter how you sit, some important part of you is uncovered. Something about the way you are in a hospital diminishes you. You can go in there the highest-class person in the world, and in ten minutes you're as undignified as a baby and totally dependent. This is not to say that hospital personnel don't care properly for their patients. It's just part of being sick.

David also describes the despondency that comes to the heart of a sick individual. He confesses that he refused to believe the truth, that he had complained, "All men are liars" (v.11). Some hospitalized people are so distraught that they no longer believe they're being told the truth. They are so dependent and despondent they can believe only *bad*. When someone comes and says, "Well, you're looking better today," they say, "No, I'm not. I'm not looking better. No one tells me the truth.

You're trying to keep something from me, to protect me from the ultimate hurt."

One of the problems Christians who suffer have is the mental and emotional flogging they give themselves while they're ill. If there's any one question that people ask me when I visit them in the hospital or talk to them about their illness, it's this: "What have I done? Oh, God, what have I done to be in this place? Why is God dealing with me in such a way? Why has God brought this sickness to my life? What does God have against me?"

And then they go back into their history and dredge up all the things they've done that they shouldn't have. They come to the conclusion that God is dealing with them harshly now because twenty years ago they were involved in A, ten years ago they did B, then there was C, and so on. All past mistakes, indiscretions, sins come back to their minds. That's a message from Satan, you know; it's not from God.

Joyce Landorf's *Mourning Song* is the best book dealing with grief and death that I've ever read. She talks about some of the struggles people experience as a family when they face the pain of losing one of their family members. In one chapter she takes up this whole matter of remembering sin and using it to flog ourselves. We let ourselves believe that it's because of our sin that we're suffering. Landorf uses a poem to illustrate this very human tendency and how we should deal with it:

I made a lash of my remembered sins.
I wove it firm and strong, with cruel tip,
And though my quivering flesh shrank from the
* scourge,*
With steady arm I plied the ruthless whip.

For surely I, who had betrayed my Lord,
Must needs endure this sting of memory.
But though my stripes grew sore, there came no peace,
And so I looked again to Calvary.

His tender eyes beneath the crown of thorns
Met mine; His sweet voice said, "My child, although
those oft-remembered sins of thine have been
like crimson scarlet, they are now like snow."

My blood, shed here, has washed them all away,
And there remained not the least dark spot,
Nor any memory of them; and so
Should you remember sins which God forgot?"

I stood there trembling, bathed in light, though scarce
My tired heart dared to hope. His voice went on:
"Look at thy feet, My child." I looked, and lo,
The whip of my remembered sins was gone![3]

One of the most difficult things for us Christians—
who have been taught from the Word of God about His
goodness, blessing, and provision—is to accept the fact

that sometimes, for no reason other than our benefit and His glory, He allows difficult problems to enter our lives. Charles Swindoll, in his book *Three Steps Forward, Two Steps Back*,[4] speaks of four spiritual flaws—a parody, of course, on Campus Crusade's four spiritual laws. One of the spiritual *flaws* Swindoll points out is this: God never allows problems to come into the lives of people who are living godly lives. And rightly he points out that the Bible does not teach that.

If you are suffering, if you are sick, if you're going through difficult times, it could be because of sin. That is possibility. But more probably it is because God loves you enough to want you to be all you can be, and He's taking you through some training to make you mature in faith. The Bible says, "Whom the Lord loves, He chastens" (Hebrews 12:6). God's dealing in our lives is evidence of His love for us, recognition that we are His children. He is making us more like Himself.

A final characteristic of sickness seen in Psalm 116 is dread. Just as David speaks twice in this psalm of the fear of death as part of his experience, never does a person with a serious illness go into the hospital without death, the ultimate dread, on his or her mind. We're put together in such a way humanly that when we are seriously ill, we carry it as far as we can. We assume the worst. David does that in this psalm, saying, "O Lord, I implore you, deliver my soul!" (v.4). All the feelings expressed by David hundreds of years ago are as up-to-date as the closest hospital. Anyone who's suffered or been sick will tell you that the emotions described in this psalm have been in their lives in some way or other. And anyone who has gone through a serious illness or other kind of suffering with a loved one, watching, serving, waiting, experiencing the emotions of helplessness, despair, and personal grief that result, suffers an aloneness that is just as traumatic and just as painful. He or she also is likely to cry out "O Lord, I implore You, deliver *all of us*!"

Bill Cearbaugh, a friend of mine, had such an experience with his wife's illness. She suffered for many months with leukemia and Bill, although he was not physically ill, suffered greatly because of her illness. After her death he wrote an account of her loneliness and his. With his permission, we are quoting a part of it here.

Looking back on all of our situation, I especially remember when Rhonda got sicker and eventually had to go to the hospital. Unconsciously, I began becoming more and more removed from her. Often, as I went to the hospital thinking that I really wanted to serve her, I would let her try to sleep and not talk to her and be quiet. I isolated myself more and more by grabbing magazines at the lobby and reading them, one after the other. Communication broke to the point where we hardly knew one another. She was getting so ill that she was finally put in a single room, by herself, and many times I would try to let her sleep by going to the lounge.

I later realized that my motive probably wasn't

one of servanthood, but I just wanted to be removed from the situation. Because of her physical state, it became more and more difficult for me, as a husband, to really love her in the way I should. By then she had lost all of her hair, she had lost several pounds in weight, and she had been in bed so long that she had a number of bed sores. Her body was very white, with almost the look of death. Her eyes were sunken in and her face looked as though she had not eaten for several days. The taste buds of her tongue were beginning to drop off. A yellow film began to develop on her teeth, and her gums were bright red and highly infected. To complicate matters the contraptions that were hanging out of her body—the intravenous tubes, the vacuum tubes drawing fluid from her lungs, and the oxygen tubes going into her nose to help her breathe—all made it very difficult for me to enjoy being around her.

I think the other reason I began withdrawing from Rhonda was that I became deeply concerned about our son's state. It became difficult to choose whether to be around John and make sure he was getting my attention or to be with Rhonda who desperately needed my attention also. I didn't realize I was violating a basic biblical principle at the time, that is that my spouse is a higher priority than my family. I can't even begin to imagine the loneliness that Rhonda must have experienced as I became more and more alienated from her. I think now of the emotions going through her heart, lying in bed in a dark single room, experiencing constant fever, unable to control her bowels and hearing the constant noise of the fluid being pulled from her lungs by the vacuum hose. The only interruptions were made by a nurse when she came to get the vital signs.

I later found out from a friend who talked to Rhonda that Rhonda felt as though she had been left alone to die and no one really cared. Even though every day the family was around to help her and encourage her and share with her from the Word and pray with her, she still sensed inwardly that we were withdrawing from her.

The remarkable part about this story, I think, is that though Rhonda had a deep, growing relationship with Christ, and was continually developing it until the day she died, in the midst of that relationship she still experienced loneliness in her own life as she was dying.

Oh, that some day I won't be left alone to die.

Notice that Psalm 116 is not a statement of despair. It is a song of praise, and it tells us how to respond to the intense loneliness caused by suffering. We are to pray:

He has heard my voice and my supplications.

(v.1)

He has inclined His ear to me. (v.2)

God is available. David cried to the Lord, and the Lord heard him. David said, "That's where I was; I cried for God; I reached out for Him." And three things happened: God heard. God helped. God healed.

God Hears

A four-year-old girl was injured, but for hours after she didn't cry. Not until her mother came home, did the child begin to sob. Someone who was watching and had been aware of her injuries said, "But why didn't you cry when you got hurt?" She answered, "Because there was nobody to cry to."

If you're a Christian, there's Somebody to cry to. That Someone is the Lord. He hears and He is not a dispassionate listener. He's an intense listener.

> *I love the Lord, because He has heard*
> *My voice and my supplications.*
> *Because He has inclined His ear to me.*
> *Therefore I will call upon Him as long as I live.*
>
> (v. 1–2)

We are never alone in our aloneness. He is there with us listening.

God Helps

Not only did God hear David's cries, He helped him.

Return to your rest, O my soul,
For the Lord has dealt bountifully with you.

(v.7)

Bountifully is a wonderful word. It means that when we cry out to God, there is always more in His hand than we asked for. I don't understand that, but I believe it's true. The way God answers our cries may not be exactly what we asked for, but it will be gracious, righteous, and merciful; and it will always be better than we imagined. It will always mean more in the viewpoint of eternity than anything you could hope for. God will help you.

God Heals

You have delivered my soul from death. . . .
I will walk before the Lord
In the land of the living. (v.8–9)

One summer while I was on vacation, I had the privilege of attending the Ocean City Bible Conference. On this particular Sunday, Anthony Campolo, an Italian sociologist and theologian, was talking about the common idea that it is the purpose of God to heal everyone from sickness. And he described some of the hurt such a philosophy brings on people: If they aren't healed, they must not have enough faith or something is wrong with them so that God won't heal them.

Campolo explained that the real problem with that philosophy is: God does not desire, it is not His purpose, to heal everyone.

"But I want to tell you something, folks," Campolo said. "It is God's purpose to heal everybody."

I thought, "What's going on? God's purpose is to heal everyone? He's just contradicted himself."

"He heals some here," Campolo continued, "and he heals some up there."

That is why David included verse 15 in Psalm 116. It says,

> *Precious in the sight of the Lord*
> *Is the death of his saints.*

Ultimately He's going to heal everyone—all the believers. Up there He will make us perfect, all we can't be here. So when a Christian faces death—separation of the soul from the body, separation from this life into the next—we hold to God's promise that He will make that person whole and perfect in the life that is eternal with Him.

David said, "I cried and He heard. I cried and He helped. I cried and He healed."

At the end of the psalm David acknowledges that we

have a personal responsibility to respond to the bounty
we receive from God. He asks, "What shall I render to the
Lord for all His benefits toward me?" (v. 12). And four
times he says, "This is what I will do."

Number one: I will remember my promises to Him.

I will pay my vows to the Lord
Now in the presence of all His people. (v. 14, 18)

Have you ever noticed how many promises you make to
God when you're hurting? "Oh, God get me out of this
mess, and I'll do thus and so and this and that." But isn't
it surprising how quickly we forget what promises we
made when we were in trouble? David said, "I'm going
to remember my promises to God."

Number two: I will show my love for God.

I will call upon Him as long as I live. (v.2)

In the midst of this situation, though I don't understand
it at all, I'm going to love God. I'm going to express my
love to Him.

Number three: I will be thankful to God.

I will offer to You the sacrifice of thanksgiving,
And will call upon the name of the Lord. (v. 17)

Throughout this study of loneliness, we have focused on one word more than any other, the word *gratitude*, and the question "*Can I as a lonely person be grateful?* " More than any other attitude, gratitude dispels from a person's heart the darkness of loneliness. In our experiences of suffering, the one thing that will help us more than anything else is to look beyond the difficulties and gratefully acknowledge that we have much in Christ Jesus.

Number four: I will put my trust in Him.

> *I will take up the cup of salvation,*
> *And call upon the name of the Lord.*
>
> (v.13)

In the years of ministry God has given me, I have learned that God can take tragedy and sorrow and use it as an arrow to the heart of a person who does not yet know Him—to cause that person to look beyond his or her own self and recognize that something is missing in that life. Facing sickness, tragedy, death, we can come alive spiritually.

Q. What can you do to help lonely sufferers
around you?

Q. Aside from deeds, are there any words you can
use to comfort sufferers?

Q. How can you prevent a sufferer from
becoming depressed?

Q. What can we do to overcome suffering?

Q. How do you deal with someone who believes that
his or her illness is a punishment?

Q. How can you comfort someone who is, or believes
he or she is, dying?

Q. How should a Christian respond to
intense loneliness?

Q. Explain this statement: "Even though you feel
alone, you are not alone."

Q. How does God deal "bountifully" with those who
pray to Him?

Chapter 8

Lonely Survivors

Ten years ago my sister Polly and I decided to live together. We had both lost our husbands and were lonely. We got a little house together and worked things out so that we were quite happy. We helped each other and shared in everything. Polly never learned to drive, so I drove her everywhere she needed to go. I never liked to cook, but Polly was a wonderful cook. We liked to do the same things and we went everywhere together.

Everything was fine until we learned Polly had cancer and that her situation was so serious the doctors could do nothing to help her. She died.

I am devastated. I am so lonely and I miss Polly so much. I don't think I can ever get over my loss. No one can replace Polly.

I couldn't stand to live alone in our house with all those memories of Polly. The house seemed so big for just me, and everything we had made me think of her. I was so sad and lonely there, I sold the house and everything that reminded me of her, and moved to an apartment complex for retired people. I thought I would find many people here who would distract me from my thoughts of Polly and help me forget.

But it hasn't worked. There are 800 people living in this complex and they are all lonely too. If my children would just call me more often, if I were younger and had more opportunities for the rest of my life, if only Polly hadn't died . . .

I wish I had gone first.

This woman, Vera, is a survivor, someone who was left behind. Some say survivors are the lucky ones, but Vera doesn't think she is so lucky. She feels abandoned—abandoned by her children, who live out of town and call every other week, abandoned by her husband who died, abandoned by her sister, Polly, who also died. She feels her life is over, that there is nothing left to live for.

The kind of struggle Vera is having is not unique to seniors. There are younger survivors who must learn to cope too.

I was the envy of all my friends. My husband and I had a lovely new home that had been professionally decorated, a swimming pool, a hot tub, and a Jaguar. The future looked bright and promising and I couldn't imagine being happier. But instead of seeing all my dreams come true, I became a widow at age 32 when my husband suffered a fatal heart attack.

I feel cheated. My life is over when it was just beginning. I still have my beautiful house and all the other things, but I would gladly trade everything to have my husband back. But he can't come back and no one can ever replace him. I know I'll never get over losing him. There's nothing left for me to live for.

Survivors seem to suffer a great deal. They feel there is no relief or comfort. Life looks bleak and empty. But friends and society tell them they need to pick up the pieces, get their grief under control, and get on with their lives. One widow said, "They give you three months to a year, and then they want you to get over it." The pressure to heal your grief, to "get over it," sometimes seems so great that survivors feel guilty for mourning and the guilt only increases their aloneness.

But mourning is a healthy process. It is something survivors must do in order to survive. Still, no one can determine a proper period for mourning. It may take the young widow five years to recover from her grief while Vera may recover in two years, or it could work for them the other way around.

Fortunately time does help in the healing process, but time alone cannot heal loneliness. For true comfort we must turn to the Master Healer.

Christ, the Master Healer

The apostle Peter gives us the promise of healing when we turn to Christ, "Who Himself bore our sins in His own body on the tree, that we, having died to sins, might live for righteousness—by whose stripes you were healed. For you were like sheep going astray, but have now returned to the Shepherd and Overseer of your souls" (1Peter 2:24–25).

We are comforted by the knowledge that because of our Savior's lonely suffering and death and His glorious resurrection, we also will rise again to have eternal life in heaven. Even when our loved ones die and leave us behind, we can become true survivors in Christ and not be overwhelmed by the pain of separation and aloneness, for we are not forever separated from them nor are we ever truly alone. Our Savior is always with us and through His power we know that the death of an earthly body is not the end of life, but the beginning of eternal happiness. Knowing this gives us comfort.

Christ, the Great Survivor

Our society does know about survivors. In fact, we admire survivors and make them our heroes. They show up in our literature and in our movies. The most admired are our mythical heroes, the ones who are always alone, the mavericks, the wanderers, the ones who ride into town at sunrise and ride out at sunset all alone, having experienced the loss of a close friend or a loved one and heroically overcome the tragedy. James Bond, Batman, Rambo, and Luke Skywalker are examples of modern day popular heroes, all of whom go through struggle and pain and suffer terrible losses. And people envy them and want to emulate them. Children buy Batman toys and Star Wars sets; they line up to see the movies, and imagine that they too could overcome such struggles.

It's strange, isn't it, that popular culture has glorified suffering, that we look on suffering as heroic. But these heroes are not real and neither is their suffering. When the story is finished or the film has run out, their suffering is over, the grieving is finished. Perhaps that is why we are unable to deal with real pain and often have no idea of how to find comfort.

Christ is our ultimate hero. He has suffered more than any human being has. And, unlike the heroes of the silver screen, He is real and His suffering is very real.

On the cross He cried out, "My God, My God, why have you forsaken Me?" (Mark 15:34) In His loneliness, He understands our pain. Because Christ suffered so much, He is the greatest survivor of all. Because Christ suffered for us, we can find comfort in Him. Because He cares for us, no matter what we experience, we are never alone—He is always with us, ready to comfort us, ready to take our loneliness from us and give us peace.

Christ, the God of All Comfort

Just as our society would like suffering to be heroic and visible grieving to end quickly, society also encourages those who have lost a loved one to retreat within themselves until they have recovered. Jane's experience is a good example. She and Sarah were good friends and visited each other every day. But when Jane, who was divorced, lost her only daughter in a car accident, Sarah stopped visiting. She thought Jane needed to be alone.

"That is what I needed least," Jane says. "At that time I needed the support of friends. I needed someone to love me in spite of my grieving."

Sometimes—in fact, much of the time—friends leave survivors alone because they don't know what to say. Thinking they should be able to say something that will quickly help the struggling survivor feel better—to stop crying, to smile and laugh, to forget the loss—and not knowing how to do that, they withdraw. They leave survivors alone to meditate on their sorrow in privacy.

"When my friend John lost his wife," says Bob, "I didn't know what to say or how to console him. I left that for others, like his kids." But there were no others. For some time, Bob's children had been distant from him, and they had their spouses to console them. Bob was alone with his grief. All alone the grief looms large and becomes overpowering.

We need to remember that people who are hurting need the support of other people. Just being there, even

when you don't know what to say, helps relieve the loneliness. Survivors sometimes need just to talk about their
loved ones and to express their loneliness and pain. Our
being willing to listen can help them.

Often the survivors seek and find solace in each
other. There is a story in the Bible of two women, both
survivors who found solace together.

> A certain man of Bethlehem, Judah, went to live in
> the country of Moab, he and his wife and his two
> sons. The name of the man was Elimelech, the name
> of his wife was Naomi . . . Then Elimelech, Naomi's
> husband, died; and she was left, and her two sons . . .
> Then both Mahlon and Chilion also died; so the
> woman survived her two sons and her husband.
>
> (Ruth 1:1–5)

Naomi told her two daughters-in-law to leave her,
return to their homes, and seek other husbands. One
daughter-in-law returned to her home, but the other,
Ruth, stayed with Naomi and comforted her. It seems
that Ruth was still young and was also beautiful. She
would certainly have found a new husband if she had
returned to her family. Perhaps she would have quickly
recovered from her own loss. But she chose not to leave
Naomi alone in her sorrow. This story is one of the most
beautiful and loving stories of the Bible, and it demon-
strates that the sharing of sorrow helps with healing.

The Bible records the stories of other survivors whose

experiences show us how to cope with personal loss. One biblical survivor is Job, whose experience was so painful, so tragic, that we would wonder how he survived it, how he could live with such terrible loss and suffering. When we read in the Bible about what happened to Job and how he survived all the tragedies, in our minds he takes on some of the qualities of the mythical heroes we often admire, and we begin to feel that his experiences were not real in the ways that ours are.

But Job was a real person and his suffering caused him real pain. He survived by praising God. Job had everything, including seven sons and three daughters and much wealth. He "feared God and shunned evil" (Job 1:1). He was "the greatest of all the people of the East" (v.3). But Job lost all of it. And how did he react? He didn't say, "I'm strong; I can handle anything. Suffering doesn't bother me." He said, "Lord I praise You for Your constant care."

> While he was still speaking, another came and said, "Your sons and daughters were eating and drinking wine in their oldest brother's house, and suddenly a great wind came from across the wilderness and struck the four corners of the house, and it fell on the young men, and they are dead." Then Job arose, tore his robe, and shaved his head; and he fell to the ground and worshipped. And he said,

"Naked I came from my mother's womb,
And naked shall I return there.
The Lord gave, and the Lord has taken away;
Blessed be the name of the Lord."

In all this Job did not sin or charge God with wrong.

(Job 1:18–22)

Praising God in time of adversity, as Job did, is one of the toughest things, and not everyone can do it. Often, when things aren't going well, people want to blame God for their problems. But Job didn't; he kept a balanced attitude, which saw him through some terrible times.

As with Job, sometimes the loss of a loved one proves to be a testing of the spirit. Through the pain, the survivor is strengthened and matures, and is better prepared to handle other problems. The Bible tells us that God comforts us in our troubles so that we may be able to comfort others.

Blessed be the God and Father of our Lord Jesus Christ, the Father of mercies and God of all comfort, who comforts us in all our tribulation, that we may be able to comfort those who are in any trouble, with the comfort with which we ourselves are comforted by God.

(2 Corinthians 1:3–4)

Receiving God's comfort and mercy ourselves enables us to comfort others.

Loneliness and Grief

Everyone experiences some kind of loneliness at some time. It may be from having to spend a Sunday afternoon alone or sitting at home on a Saturday night feeling abandoned. No matter how strong you believe you are, these feelings will come to you, even if you stay very busy so that you think loneliness hardly has a chance to touch you. But for some, loneliness has become an ever present condition.

According to Katherine Barrett, in an article published in *Ladies' Home Journal*, loneliness has become prevalent in American society. "The figures tell a poignant tale," Barrett says. Half of today's marriages will end in divorce, and the majority of married women will eventually end up widows"[1] Almost fifty percent of women over the age of sixty-five are widows.

We are living in lonely times where single survivors— the survivors of death, divorce, war, and old age—have become the majority. It is no wonder that loneliness has become an epidemic. And these lonely people will do anything to relieve their loneliness.

According to Barrett, there are two distinct kinds of loneliness. "The less intense variety is tied to a lack of community or network of friends; the more anguishing comes from the lack or loss of an intimate tie." The most troubling aspect, says Barrett, is that loneliness is dangerous. "The divorced and widowed have much higher mortality rates than the general population," and these people "are much more self-destructive."[2] Lonely survivors experience the most intense form of loneliness and feel they will always remain lonely. Their loneliness becomes despair, and they feel hopeless.

Psychologists tell us that people must cope with loneliness and that by coping they will overcome it. "The truth is that most people are not lonely forever," says Dr. Carin Rubenstein, "although they think they will be. It's like depression; you think you'll always be that way."[3]

We know that all of us need to work toward maintaining positive attitudes, but, even though it's hard to be positive when you are lonely, survivors especially need to in order to survive. Many who struggle to survive feel like they are in Antarctica while everyone else is sunning themselves in Florida. It's hard to feel sunny and warm while facing the cold world of harsh reality all alone.

Dana and her husband, Bob, moved into a new apartment in suburbia. Then Bob died in an industrial accident at work.

After Bob died, I couldn't bear to go through the day. I'd come home to my apartment, and all was so quiet.

I'd notice how neat and untouched everything looked. I'd cook a dinner for only one person. I had no one to argue with about what television program

I'd watch. Then I'd get into my double bed and cry. I
missed him so much. I felt nothing could fill that void.

In her apartment, Dana felt cut off from everything.
Since she was new to the area, she didn't know many
neighbors. Those she did know were mainly college students. She had no one to confide in and give her comfort.

Dana recognized she needed to belong to something,
that she needed to reach out.

I just wanted someone I could talk to. So I decided I
should go back to church.

And she found more than she had expected. As she was
welcomed into the church community, she not only found
friends that she could talk to, she also found faith in Christ
and renewed hope. Finally she had something to look forward to and contact with people who made her feel needed.

I stopped thinking about me all the time, and about
how bad I had it. I began to think of others. I was
appointed Sunday school director. I felt needed. They
gave me responsibility; I felt I had a purpose in life.

Dana found she could overcome her loneliness in
the Lord Jesus and in service to others. To feel needed
and have a sense of belonging can do wonders to create
a positive attitude.

I also discovered that my life wasn't really my own,
but was one to be shared with others. I found I had
to take that first step and not worry about rejection.

Many people remain lonely because they fear rejection.
Like Dana they are reluctant to reach out for friendship
and comfort. They think rejection hurts worse than loneliness and spend much of their time and money trying to
avoid it. But that is a wrong attitude. Those who expect
to be rejected usually will feel that they are. Those who
expect to receive friendship and comfort usually will.

Christ says,

Ask, and it will be given to you;

Seek, and you will find; knock and it will be
opened to you. For everyone who asks receives, and
he who seeks finds, and to him who knocks it will be
opened . . . Whatever you want men to do to you, do
also to them.

(Matthew 7:7–12)

When you need friendship and comfort, offer friendship and comfort, and don't expect rejection. Accept
yourself where you are, whatever your need, and remember that Christ will not reject you. When you reach out to
Him, He will always respond with loving acceptance. He
says, "If you then, being evil, know how to give good gifts
to your children [and your friends and all those around

you], how much more will your Father who is in heaven give good things to those who ask Him!" (v. 11)

You can become a survivor in Christ through your faith in Him. In Him, you can survive grief, and you can survive loneliness. Your greatest source of comfort and hope is Christ Jesus. And that hope can become a right spirit of praise and thanksgiving for His constant care.

War Breeds Loneliness

Another time of hardship that requires survivors to keep a right spirit rather than despair in loneliness is a time of war. War separates families. Mothers and fathers may be called away from their small children to serve their country. Spouses become separated from each other, as well as sons and daughters from their parents, and brothers from sisters.

According to Dietrich Bonhoeffer, a World War II clergyman who spent time in a concentration camp, "There is nothing that can fill the gap when we are away from those we love and . . . it would be wrong to try."[4] Although your loved ones cannot be replaced, God can indeed fill that void.

War not only tears families apart, but it breeds fear as well. During the Persian Gulf War, one recruit recorded in his diary that he was scared and alone. At the same time, his family felt a sense of loss and fear. Otis and his family members all felt a loss at being separated and not knowing what would happen. They had to learn to face the future even though they were separated and lonely.

A foreign exchange student, Ali felt loneliness during the Persian Gulf War. His family was in Kuwait, and he couldn't contact them.

> Then I learned my parents had fled to Iraq, but my brother couldn't tell me how they were or where exactly they were. Never before have I felt so alone. Even though I had friends here, it was difficult for me to confide in them. I felt I had lost everything, that my whole world had ended. No one else could really understand what I was facing.
>
> Eventually Ali was able to contact his parents who were alive but fearful, and they were unable to leave Iraq. Ali still felt terrible, being so far away from them and knowing that he could have lost them. "I realize now how precious my family is," he says.

Like all the others, Ali, a survivor, has had to learn to survive.

Biblical Survivors

The Bible tells of Joseph, who was sold into slavery by his jealous brothers. His father, Jacob, must have felt about Joseph much the same way Ali did about his loved ones:

> Then Jacob tore his clothes, put sackcloth on his waist,
> and mourned for his son many days. And all his sons
> and all his daughters arose to comfort him; but he
> refused to be comforted, and he said, "For I shall go
> down into the grave to my son in mourning." Thus his
> father wept for him. (Genesis 37:34–35)

Jacob believed Joseph was dead, but he was taken to Egypt, and even though Joseph was physically alone, the Bible says the Lord was with him (see Genesis 39:2). And because of it, Joseph was able not only to survive but to prosper. He overcame many adversities while separated from the love, companionship, and comfort of his father. He was even put in jail for a crime he did not commit. But again, the Lord was with him, and Joseph became the keeper of the prison. Whenever he found adversity, he managed to make the best of his situation. He kept a positive mental attitude. Eventually, when the pharaoh was troubled by bad dreams, Joseph was able to interpret the dreams as a sign of impending famine. He was taken out of prison and made the prime minister.

> Then Pharaoh said to Joseph, "Inasmuch as God has
> shown you all this, there is no one as discerning and
> wise as you. You shall be over my house, and all my
> people shall be ruled according to your word."
> (Genesis 41:39–40)

Joseph kept his faith and did not give in to adversity or loneliness. He learned to be a survivor.

Abraham had many adversities to overcome, and he also survived. Abraham and Sarah were too old to have children but wanted them badly. God gave them Isaac, a child who was very precious to Abraham. Then God asked Abraham to give Him the ultimate sacrifice, his son Isaac.

How many parents could even think of making such a sacrifice? Most would refuse and turn away from God. But Abraham's faith in God's goodness was strong, and he prepared to follow God's direction. The Lord sent an angel to stop Abraham from killing Isaac, and even he marveled at Abraham's unquestioning faith. But Abraham knew that God's promise, power, and provision were greater than his own personal needs.

Think of what must have been going through Abraham's mind. Imagine the thoughts he had of the pain he would suffer at the loss of the child he had waited for so long. But he trusted God. He believed that no matter how bad the situation seemed, God would care for him. He was willing to do God's will no matter what the cost.

Sooner or later, we all face the reality of human loss. You may lose a mate, a friend, a job, a position, or security, status, or wealth. But you will never lose the gift of eternal life. The Bible promises, "The sufferings of this present time are not worthy to be compared with the glory which shall be revealed in us" (Romans 8:18).

In reality, you are never alone if Christ is with you. You share in all that He is, and all that He has. Life is more than a struggle to survive. For the Christian, it is an exciting adventure with the living God.

Q. How can you help someone overcome his or her intense grief while mourning for a loved one?

Q. What comforts do we have when we are lonely?

Q. Rather than popular heroes, to whom should we turn as an example?

Q. What biblical examples can we turn to in order to comfort ourselves or a friend?

Q. How can we keep a good mental attitude in times of adversity?

Q. Is it possible for the loss of a loved one to be the testing of your spirit?

Q. How can people overcome the fear of rejection when reaching out to others for help?

Q. What organizations should people turn to for help?

Q. How does war separate families?

Q. How can we follow the examples of biblical people such as Job or Joseph in overcoming loneliness?

Chapter 9

The Lonely Savior

Then Jesus came with them to a place called Gethsemane, and said to the disciples, "Sit here while I go and pray over there." And He took with Him Peter and the two sons of Zebedee, and He began to be sorrowful and deeply distressed. Then He said to them, "My soul is exceedingly sorrowful, even to death. Stay here and watch with me."

He went a little farther and fell on His face, and prayed, saying, "O My Father, if it is possible, let this cup pass from Me; nevertheless, not as I will, but as You will." Then He came to the disciples and found them sleeping, and said to Peter, "What! Could you not watch with Me one hour? Watch and pray, lest you enter into temptation. The spirit indeed is willing, but the flesh is weak."

Again, a second time He went away and prayed, saying, "O My Father, if this cup cannot pass away from Me unless I drink it, Your will be done." And He came and found them asleep again, for their eyes were heavy. So He left them, went away again, and prayed the third time, saying the same words.

Then He came to his disciples and said to them, "Are you still sleeping and resting? Behold, the hour is at hand, and the Son of Man is being betrayed into the hands of sinners. Rise, let us be going. See, My betrayer is at hand."

(Matthew 26:36–46)

And about the ninth hour Jesus cried out with a loud voice, saying, "Eli, Eli, lama sabachthani?" that is, "My God, My God, why have You forsaken Me?"

(Matthew 27:46)

The King of Kings came into the world humbly. He was born in a stable, His cradle a feed trough. In His thirty-two years of earthly life, He owned no possessions. He had to depend on others to provide for His needs, and He had to borrow everything He used. The stable where He was born was borrowed. He borrowed money to pay His taxes, a boat to stand in and preach, and a cross on which to die. Even His tomb was not his own.

But He had a mission that He alone could accomplish: He, the Son of Man, came to "seek and to save that which was lost" (Luke 19:10). He bore our sins "in His own body on the tree" that in the age to come we might have eternal life (see 1 Peter 2:24, Mark 10:29–30, and John 3:13–17). Of Himself He says, "I am the resurrection and the life. He who believes in Me, though he may die, he shall live. And whoever lives and believes in Me shall never die" (John 11:25–26). He "put away sin by the sacrifice of Himself . . . so Christ was offered once to bear the sins of many. . . . We have been sanctified through the offering of the body of Jesus Christ once for all" (Hebrews 9:26–10:10).

We know these things and we praise Him for our salvation through His death, burial, and resurrection, for His glorious triumph over death and hell. We are overwhelmed that because He loves us so much, a love we know we don't deserve, He would sacrifice Himself for us. But when we think of His life on earth, we find it hard to think of our Savior as lonely.

After all, He was God on earth. He was perfect, blameless, without sin. He was in the beginning when God formed the earth and us. He knew why He came and He knew what would happen. He had always known how He would live on earth and how He would die. How could He be lonely? Why would the things that cause pain to us cause pain to Him? Wouldn't He be above all that?

He was God in human form. His body needed food, rest, and shelter, and his human spirit needed companionship. When something injured His body, He felt pain. When something injured His human spirit, He felt rejection, despair, and loneliness. Because His mission was so great, the loneliness it caused Him was also great, greater than anyone else has ever known. He felt the loneliness of suffering. He felt abandoned and rejected by the very people He came into the world to save. In His greatest moments of human despair, He even felt abandoned by God, His own Father.

Being alone is not the same as being lonely. When you are alone, you are independent. When you are lonely, you feel isolated, cut off.

Everyone feels lonely at one time or another. Jean-Paul Sartre, an existentialist philosopher, attempting to express his own feelings of futility, loneliness, and abandonment, said, "We are isolated from others, from past and future, from meaning and value. We can count on nobody but ourselves, because we are alone, abandoned on earth, and without help. Life is absurd and love is impossible. So, we are condemned to futility in an impersonal world and in a universe with neither heart nor meaning."[1]

But Sartre had it all wrong. We are not isolated from meaning and value; we are not abandoned in an impersonal universe. We do have someone to count on. We have our Lord Jesus Christ who gives meaning and purpose to our lives. Our Savior took on Himself the suffering of the world. He alone bore our pain and loneliness. He gives heart to a very personal world and the promise of an eternal future.

Christ's Ministry

As a child, Jesus was set apart. No other child was His peer. He thought differently from other children. Even when He was very young, He knew He had to do the work of His Father in heaven, and He began to prepare. He went to Jerusalem with His earthly parents; and when they began the journey home, Jesus stayed behind. He went into the temple to learn from the elders. When Mary and Joseph found Him there, after searching for Him for three days, they rebuked Him for having worried them, for being in the temple instead of with them. But Jesus said to them, "Why did you seek Me? Did you not know that I must be about My Father's business?" (Luke 2:49)

Jesus began His ministry by fasting alone in the wilderness for forty days. The Bible tells us that He was led by the Spirit to be tempted by the devil (see Matthew 4:1–2) and that afterward He was hungry.

> Now when the tempter came to Him, he said, "If You are the Son of God, command that these stones become bread." But He answered and said, "It is written, 'Man shall not live by bread alone, but by every word that proceeds from the mouth of God.'"
>
> (Matthew 4:3–4)

Jesus' rebuke of Satan means that although you will be tempted and feel alone, you can find solace and help in God's Word.

The devil tried to tempt Jesus two more times until Jesus said to him,

> Away with you, Satan! For it is written, "You shall worship the Lord your God, and Him only you shall serve."
>
> (Matthew 4:10)

We must always remember that God's Word stands alone and that God is the only god we worship. When we worship Him, when we seek solace in His word, He will comfort us just as He comforted the Son of Man when His struggle with temptation was ended.

> Then the devil left Him, and behold, angels came and ministered to Him.
>
> (Matthew 4:11)

God the Father created the world and everything in it. When God formed Adam from the dust, Adam was alone, and he became lonely. The first man needed the companionship of another person. Christ also began His ministry alone. John the Baptist prepared the way for Him, but John was imprisoned and ultimately killed. Jesus was still alone when He went to Galilee to preach and teach.

At this time Jesus called out twelve disciples.

> And He went up on the mountain and called to Him those He Himself wanted. And they came to Him.

> Then He appointed twelve, *that they might be with Him* and that He might send them out to preach, and to have power to heal sicknesses and to cast out demons.
>
> (Mark 3:13–15)

Even though He chose twelve disciples, who not only were His companions but also His students and helpers in training to spread the Gospel, Jesus walked a lonely path. He was the Son of God, unerring and perfect. His disciples were sinners capable of doubt and error. They were incapable of empathizing with Him or of even a partial understanding of the anguish He would experience. Neither could they fully grasp His teaching.

> When He had called the multitude to Himself, He said to them, "Hear and understand: Not what goes into the mouth defiles a man; but what comes out of the mouth, this defiles a man. . . . Every plant which My heavenly Father has not planted will be uprooted. Let [the Pharisees] alone. They are blind leaders of the blind. And if the blind leads the blind, both will fall into a ditch."
>
> Then Peter answered and said to Him, "Explain this parable to us."
>
> So Jesus said, "Are you also still without understanding?"
>
> (Matthew 15:10–16)

One source of the feeling of isolation is to find you are not understood. Not only were His companions unable to understand Jesus' teaching, they didn't comprehend His warnings of betrayal.

> From that time Jesus began to show to His disciples that He must go to Jerusalem, and suffer many things from the elders and chief priests and scribes and be killed, and be raised again the third day.
>
> Then Peter took Him aside and began to rebuke Him, saying, "Far be it from You, Lord; this shall not happen to You!"
>
> (Matthew 16:21–22)

> For He taught His disciples and said to them, "The Son of Man is being betrayed into the hands of men, and they will kill Him. And after He is killed, He will rise the third day." But they did not understand this saying, and were afraid to ask Him.
>
> (Mark 9:31–32)

> Then He took the twelve aside and said to them, "Behold, we are going up to Jerusalem, and all things that are written by the prophets concerning the Son of Man will be accomplished . . ." But they understood none of these things.
>
> (Luke 18:31–34)

Christ did all this and bore all this alone. Even for you the road to heaven could be a lonely one. Faith in God does not guarantee you a path of popularity or guarantee tons of friends. Although Jesus had the love and adoration of many, He had to abandon friends, followers, His earthly mother, and all earthly things to do God's will.

The Rejected Lord

While our Savior, the incarnate Son of God, was on this earth, He put Himself at the mercy of friends and foes. He taught of God's love, the way to salvation, and eternal life. But He was rejected. The scribes and Pharisees spoke against Him. What did He do to deserve that? He healed the sick and lame and preached God's Word. He did what was right and kind, but the Jewish leaders rejected Him. And one of His disciples, Judas, turned against Him as well.

Now, think about it. How can a perfect person receive such negative reactions from people? Perhaps it is because the world itself it imperfect. People don't always recognize the truth when they hear it. They follow false prophets and are misled by worldly things.

A part of loneliness is feeling the world is against you. Many people feel they have no friends. And they feel people have turned against them. Imagine how Christ must have felt. Not only were the Jewish leaders against Him, but all the forces of evil on earth as well. The Pharisees accused Jesus of being evil.

> But the Pharisees said, "He casts out demons by the
> ruler of the demons." (Matthew 9:34)

Harriet Hohreiter thinks we should look at the Savior as an example when we feel lonely, sad, or rejected—especially when we feel abandoned by the world. She says, "He is the most perfect Being on earth, and they crucified Him. Why should you feel all alone? Why should you feel so abandoned by friends? Loneliness is not a fault in you. If Christ felt it, why should you feel so upset?"

Her advice makes sense. Many people feel they are lonely through some defect in personality. Yet Christ is the most perfect Being, and He, too, experienced loneliness and rejection. Jesus knew His fate would be a lonely one, and He would have to leave those on earth. He said,

> Can the friends of the bridegroom mourn as long as
> the bridegroom is with them? But the days will come
> when the bridegroom will be taken away from them,
> and then they will fast.
>
> (Matthew 9:15)

Although Jesus walked alone in His mission, suffered alone, was rejected by the world, and denied by His friends, our lonely Savior had consolation. His heavenly Father was with Him.

> And yet if I do judge, My judgment is true; for I am
> not alone, but I am with the Father who sent me.
>
> (John 8:16)

Even though Jesus might have felt alone at times like we do, He knew He had a Father in heaven who would be with Him.

> And He who sent Me is with Me. The Father has not left Me alone, for I always do those things that please Him. (John 8:29)

Christ promises that people can find peace in Him:

> Come to Me, all you who labor and are heavy laden, and I will give you rest. (Matthew 11:28)

Our Savior promises that He can relieve people's burdens even the burden of loneliness. He has conquered loneliness for us by His death on the cross.

Throughout His ministry, Jesus met doubters as well as faithful followers. That's to be expected. But, on occasion, even His disciples had doubts. That must have hurt the most. You expect opposition from some people, but you don't expect your friends to question you.

Peter tried to walk on water and began to sink. He called to Jesus for help.

> But when he saw that the wind was boisterous, he was afraid; and beginning to sink he cried out, saying, "Lord, save me!" And immediately Jesus stretched out His hand and caught him, and said to him, "O you of little faith, why did you doubt?" (Matthew 14:30–31)

In many ways Peter was our Lord's best disciple, but even Peter doubted and later denied Him. Think of how Jesus felt when His most faithful follower doubted Him.

In an article entitled "Rejection: Is It Worse Than Loneliness?" Jeannette Acrea claims people are lonely because they fear rejection. But, she says, we need to reach out to others and risk possible rejection. When Peter doubted Christ, Jesus was able, through His own confidence, to turn that doubt into faith. Can you overcome your fear of rejection and reach out to someone else?

If Jesus lived on earth today, would He be treated differently? Probably not. Human nature hasn't changed. And He is still being denied and rejected by both friends and foes. Indeed even pastors are rejecting and denying our Savior: One ordained minister who was head of a seminary was indicted for multiple counts of heresy. Jesus has it just as tough today as He had it 2,000 years ago.

In the later years of Robert Ingersoll's life, he was asked why he had stopped delivering his lecture on "The Errors and Inconsistencies of the Bible." This well known unbeliever said, "There is no need for me to do that anymore, as many preachers in the pulpits are denying the truths of the Bible in the churches of our land and are accomplishing more to destroy faith in the Bible than I could do by taking to the lecture platform."[2]

Jesus' Last Hours

At the Last Supper, Jesus again told His disciples that someone would betray Him. While they were eating He said, "Assuredly, I say unto you, one of you will betray Me" (Matthew 26:21). Nothing is more lonely than the feeling of betrayal by one of your closest friends. But Christ knew that would happen and He knew He would have to go through the most difficult moments alone. To make matters worse, He also knew that Peter would claim he didn't know Jesus for fear the soldiers might accuse him as well. He knew He had a burden to carry; who would not be tormented knowing that his life would be cut short and he would die around the age of thirty-two?

Jesus asked Peter and the two sons of Zebedee to go with Him to pray in the Garden of Gethsemane. In one of His most emotional times, He said, "My Soul is exceedingly sorrowful, even to death. Stay here and watch with Me" (Matthew 26:38). But while Jesus prayed so hard that He sweat blood, His companions fell asleep and left Him alone.

Jesus desperately wanted someone with Him, to help Him in His time of greatest need, to give Him comfort. He also understood that He alone must bear the heavy burden that He must carry. In times of loneliness and despair, people often try to reassure us of their concern. But we know we must learn to stand alone.

The most devastating remark about Gethsemane is:

"Then all the disciples forsook Him and fled" (Matthew 26:56). Jesus was betrayed, abandoned, and denied by His own disciples. He was left alone with the enemy.

But Jesus was not the only one to feel alone. Peter, after denying he knew Jesus, realized he had betrayed his Lord:

> And Peter remembered the word of Jesus who had said to him, "Before the rooster crows, you will deny Me three times." Then he went out and wept bitterly.
>
> (Matthew 26:75)

Peter is considered one of the greatest—if not the greatest—disciple. Christians of all types recognize the significance of Peter. He was one of the leaders of the early Church and played a significant role in the New Testament. Still, it's amazing to see that a man with such recognition as a holy man made mistakes and went off alone to weep. The disciples and our Savior had led lives of loneliness as well as full and meaningful lives. Even though Peter occasionally faltered in his faith, he never lost it.

After Jesus was crucified, His enemies still plotted to ruin His reputation. While He was in the grave, the Romans sealed it so Jesus' friends could not steal the body.

> Now the next day, that followed the day of the preparation, the chief priests and Pharisees came together

unto Pilate, saying, "Sir, we remember that that deceiver said, while he was yet alive, 'After three days I will rise again.' Command therefore that the sepulchre be made sure until the third day lest his disciples come by night, and steal him away, and say unto the people, 'He is risen from the dead' so the last error shall be worse than the first."

(Matthew 27:62–64 KJV)

Even in the loneliness of the tomb, Jesus had people plotting against Him. Of course, Jesus knew He would rise again as the prophets foretold. Jesus' victory over death gives us victory over death, sin, and even loneliness.

Jesus' Reassurance

Jesus' words at the end of the Book of Matthew are reassuring. He says, "And lo, I am with you always, even to the end of the age" (Matthew 28:20). These are reassuring words for Christians because Jesus is always with us as He promised in the Book of Matthew. When we are down and feel very alone, we should try to keep these words in mind.

This reminds me of a story about a little boy who came home crying after playing hide-and-seek. His father asked him why he was crying. The little boy said no one came to find him while he was hiding. "Now do you know how hurt God feels," asked the father, "when He waits for those to seek Him but they do not?"

Although God is not playing hide-and-seek games with us, He expects us to seek Him. Although there are instances in the Bible where God called people such as Jonah, Moses, or Abraham, the Scripture also tells us to seek Him while He may be found.

At times, however, God may seem to remain silent. Take for example, the child who, afraid of the dark, thought he'd prefer someone with skin on even though he knew God was with him.

God is with us, but we're often like that little boy, wanting reassurance from someone we can see or touch. When God seems silent, we must learn to exercise our faith in Him.

How We Can Use Our Faith

We can use our faith two ways: through persistence and through perspective. You must not be silent in prayer but be persistent in your prayers to God. And when we are faced with loneliness, we need to look at our situation from a different perspective. If we look at it from a different point of view, the situation probably won't seem as bad.

Christ is the only Savior of the world. But the Bible tells stories of leaders who, with God's help, "saved" their people. Moses led his people out of Egypt where they were miserable and enslaved. But after he brought the Ten Commandments down from the mountain where

God had given them to him, he saw his people sinning. He had spent days there with God only to return to find the Israelites had not listened to him or God. As a savior, he was alone, and it was his sole duty to bring his people back to God. He said, "I am not able to bear all these people alone, because the burden is too heavy for me" (Numbers 11:14). With God's help, Moses was a savior, and he too felt lonely.

Joseph saved the Hebrew people from the famine by giving them food that Egypt had stored. Joseph had spent many years alone because his brothers sold him into slavery. Joseph was also jailed for an offense of which he was not guilty. Joseph, too, had saved the Israelites by following God's orders. But his path was not an easy one; it was often a lonely one.

The Book of Lamentations says, "It is good for man that he bear the yoke in his youth. He sitteth alone and keepeth silence, because he hath borne it upon him" (3:27–28 KJV). Sometimes being alone is necessary to understand what life is all about.

Christ bore His burden alone on the cross so that He could obtain victory over death for us. According to Keith M. Doornbos, in his article "Never Abandoned," we should never misconstrue our sense of aloneness as abandonment. "Jesus Christ has suffered so that we should never be abandoned. In history's most tragic moment we find our greatest hope. With that hope we can face despair that all too quickly and unexpectedly slams into life."[3]

Doornbos is talking about those words that Christ spoke upon the cross, "My God, My God, why have You forsaken me?" Since Christ bore all the agony, loneliness, and sin of the world, we do not have to fear God's forsaking us. God will always be with us, even unto the end of the age.

Q. How can we use Jesus as an example of overcoming loneliness in our own lives?

Q. How did Jesus deal with rejection?

Q. Why did Jesus experience loneliness?

Q. How did Jesus deal with His experiences of loneliness?

Q. If Christ says He will always be with us, why do people feel lonely?

Q. How did Jesus deal with temptation?

Q. Does Jesus still experience troubles?

Q. How can we bring Jesus further into our lives?

Q. How would you react to the Jean-Paul Sartre statement, found on page 136?

Q. What promises of Jesus should we remember when feeling lonely?

Chapter 10

Loneliness in the Bible

What has happened to us? What has happened that human beings can no longer be near one another, even though we are right next to each other?

When with that thought in mind I opened the Bible and began to read, I was overwhelmed at what I found. I discovered that although the words "lonely" and "loneliness" don't appear in Scripture, the pages of the Bible are filled with illustrations of people who battled that disease.

The Reality of Loneliness

We can go back in Genesis to a man named Enoch. The Bible says he walked a path quite apart from his contemporaries. In a wicked world he stood out like a shining star on a dark night. To be set apart that way causes loneliness, but "Enoch walked with God; and he was not, for God took him" (5:24).

On the heels of Enoch came Noah, to whom God gave the "absurd" instructions to build a boat where there was no water. For many years he worked at building that huge vessel. All the while he was the subject of abuse by his contemporaries, but the Book of Hebrews tells us Noah walked by faith (see 11:7). He did what God told him to do, although he had to do it all be himself.

In Genesis 16 we read the story of Hagar, a woman who experienced loneliness. When Abraham's wife Sarah could not bear children, she gave Hagar, her Egyptian handmaid, to Abraham for a wife. Even though Sarah wanted Hagar to bear children for Abraham, she was jealous because she could not do that herself. Eventually hostility between these two women grew to a boiling point, and Sarah banished Hagar to the wilderness. As you read Hagar's story, you cannot miss the misery of her loneliness. She is away from family and friends. No one is with her—she is alone. Yet God met her at that time.

Go with me to the mountain of Moriah. There Abraham trudged up to the pinnacle with his son, Isaac, to carry out a terrible commandment from God: Take that son who is the object of your love, and the hope and the promise of the coming nation, and put him to death (see Genesis 22:2).

Abraham was completely isolated in that experience. He could not take even his servants with him. He and his son went to the mountain, and there God spoke to him redemptively.

Moses too was a man apart. We read his story in the Book of Exodus. While working in Pharaoh's court, he often took long walks by himself. On one of those walks he came across an Egyptian fighting with a Hebrew. In anger Moses murdered the Egyptian, and as a result fled into the wilderness to hide from Pharaoh. The next time we see Moses, he's wandering around on the back side of the desert, taking care of his father-in-law's sheep. Certainly during those years of his life Moses experienced loneliness, but God came to him also.

David, the psalmist, knew deep loneliness. We're indebted to him because he put into the words of his psalms the way a lonely person cries out for comfort. How descriptively David expressed his solitude.

> *For my days are consumed like smoke,*
> *And my bones are burned like a hearth.*
> *I am like a pelican of the wilderness;*
> *I am like an owl of the desert.*
> *I lie awake,*
> *And am like a sparrow alone on the housetop.*
>
> (Psalm 102:3, 6–7)

> *Reproach has broken my heart,*
> *And I am full of heaviness;*
> *I looked for someone to take pity, but there was none;*
> *And for comforters, but I found none.*
>
> (Psalm 69:20)

David expressed his loneliness in a way we can identify with, and God came to David too.

Job stands out as the extreme and supreme Old Testament example of a lonely man. Nowhere did he find a receptive response. In the midst of his suffering, he felt that even God had abandoned him. He was an island among men, confronting the pain of his being.

When we leave the paths of the Old Testament and walk into the New Testament, we are introduced almost immediately to the disciples called by the Savior to help, to encourage, and to walk with Him in His earthly ministry. As we read the story, we can feel the growing emotions of fear and anxiety that well up in them as the Savior begins to talk about His impending death. Finally they begin to accept that He really is going to die, that they are going to be deprived of His presence. They hurt with the misunderstanding that surrounds the loneliness of their knowledge, because Jesus had said He would never leave them. They understood He meant He would remain with them in the way they would be with each other. They were confused and frightened.

Early in His ministry Jesus warned His disciples, "Indeed the hour is coming, yes, has now come, that you will be scattered, each to his own, and will leave Me alone" (John 16:32). The Savior, the Christ, felt loneliness. Not only did He experience loneliness when it came, but He knew intimately that it was coming—and all the anguish that went with the anticipation of it was His as well.

We follow Him in the closing hours of His life to the Garden of Gethsemane. He took with Him three friends, and He asked them, "Will you stay here at the edge of the garden and watch and pray with Me?" Then He went into the garden and agonized over God's will—the impending judgment of sin He would carry. When He came back to His friends, He found them asleep. You cannot miss the loneliness in His words, "What, could you not watch with Me one hour?"

On Calvary our Savior experienced the greatest loneliness. One of His disciples had betrayed Him. His friends had fled. And, seemingly for an eternity, even His Father had turned away. In the agony of that hour, He cried out, "My God, My God, why have You forsaken Me?" (Matthew 27:46)

The loneliness of that moment is beyond description, but it is the guarantee that Jesus is able to understand us in our battle with that enemy.

God's Comfort to the Lonely

Genesis 16 tells us that God met Hagar in the wilderness as she waited alone by the fountain of waters. Hagar was in the wilderness by herself, and when she realized that God saw her, she named a memorial to God's awareness of a lonely person.

Abraham's experience was something like Hagar's. When he was in the depths of his lonely obedience, God met him. At the exact moment when God knew that the testing had gone far enough, He broke the silence.

But the angel of the Lord called to him from heaven and said, "Abraham, Abraham!" so he said, "Here I am." And He said, "Do not lay your hand on the lad, or do anything to him; for now I know that you fear God, since you have not withheld your son, your only son, from Me."

Then Abraham lifted his eyes and looked, and there behind him was a ram caught in a thicket by its horns. So Abraham went and took the ram, and offered it up for a burnt offering instead of his son.

(Genesis 22:11–13)

Notice what Abraham did next:

And Abraham called the name of that place Jehovah-Jireh.

(v. 14 KJV)

Jehovah-Jireh literally means "The Lord will provide." Abraham selected that name for his monument to God because the Lord had provided for him and for Isaac.

These two Old Testament monuments, Hagar's and Abraham's, testify to God's willingness to meet us when we hurt and are all alone. God also shows His care for us in the way He met with a number of other Old Testament people.

While Moses was alone in the desert, for example, God spoke to him and revealed Himself through a burning bush. He said, "I'm here! And I want you to serve me." And God called Moses into service (see Exodus 3:2–10).

God met Job in the wilderness, too. In the midst of Job's tragic life, God spoke to him out of a whirlwind. And Job was aware that God was no longer absent from him. He said, "I have heard of You by the hearing of the ear, but now my eye sees You" (Job 42:5).

David, who wrote so vividly about loneliness, also wrote about comfort:

> *The Lord is my shepherd; I shall not want . . .*
> *Yea, though I walk through the valley of the shadow of*
> *death . . .*
> *You are with me.*
>
> (Psalm 23:1–4)

> *The Lord is my light and my salvation . . .*
> *The Lord is the strength of my life;*
> *Of whom shall I be afraid?*
>
> (Psalm 27:1)

To the lonely disciples who mourned the anticipated absence of their Savior, Jesus said,

> Let not your heart be troubled; you believe in God, believe also in Me. In My Father's house are many mansions; if it were not so, I would have told you. I go to prepare a place for you.
>
> And if I go and prepare a place for you, I will come again.
>
> (John 14:1–3)

The word "comforter" comes from the Greek word *paraclete*, which means "one who stands by you." Jesus said to His disciples, "The Holy Spirit will come and *stand by you*."

The God who saw Hagar in the wilderness sees you. The God who provided for Abraham will provide for you. The God who spoke to Job speaks to you today. The Shepherd and salvation of David is your Shepherd and your salvation. The Comforter that Christ promised to the disciples is your Comforter. He will come to you.

Most of all, the Christ who experienced ultimate loneliness will provide mercy and grace to help you in times of need.

Years ago a philosopher named Seneca wrote these words in one of his epistles. Repeating them seems to be a fitting way to close this book, for they recapture all the kinds of loneliness we've been thinking about.

For who listens to us in all the world? Whether he be friend or teacher, brother or father or mother, sister or neighbor, son or ruler or servant, does he listen? Our advocate, or our husbands, or our wives—those who are dearest to us—do the stars listen when we turn desperately away from man, or the great winds, or the seas, or the mountains? To whom can any man say, "Here am I! Behold me in my nakedness, in my wounds, my secret grief, my despair, my betrayal, my pain, my tongue which cannot express my sorrow, my

terror, my abandonment! Listen to me for a day, at least
for an hour, or just for a moment." Lonely silence . . .
Oh, God, is there no one to listen?[1]

Jesus listens. Jesus will always listen. He is waiting for you
to speak to Him.

Q. When is loneliness first mentioned in the Bible?

Q. How do the men and women of the Bible handle rejection while doing the will of God?

Q. Do the Old Testament men and women differ in problems or solutions from those in the New Testament?

Q. How can we apply the biblical examples to our own?

Q. How does God comfort the lonely?

Q. How can we use these biblical examples in overcoming our loneliness?

Q. How would you define the word "comforter"?

Q. Read the Book of Job. How does Job stand out as the extreme and supreme lonely man? How can we profit from his examples?

Q. How has God revealed Himself to people in the Bible?

Q. God is a provider. List friends and family He has provided for you.

Notes

Chapter 1: Loneliness—A Disease of Our Time

1. Author Unknown.

2. Miller McPherson, Lynn Smith-Lovin, and Matthew E. Brashears, "Social Isolation in America: Changes in Core Discussion Networks Over Two Decades," *American Sociological Review*, June 3, 2006, 1.

3. Craig W. Ellison, "Roots of Loneliness," *Christianity Today*, March 10, 1978.

4. James J. Lynch in an interview with Christopher Anderson, *People*, August 22, 1977, 30.

5. "The Cure for Loneliness," *Family Life: God's View of Relationships*, edited by Jean McAllister (Waco: Word Publishers, 1976), 141–142.

6. Katherine Barrett, "An Epidemic Called Loneliness," *Ladies Home Journal*, May 1983, 90.

7. Samuel Taylor Coleridge, "The Rime of the Ancient Mariner," Harvard Classics, Vol. 41 (New York: P.F. Collier and Son, 1910). 705.

8. Morris L. West, *The Devil's Advocate* (New York: Dell, 1959), 334–335.

Chapter 2: Lonely Saints

1. Joseph Bayle, "A Psalm in a Hotel Room," *Psalms of My Life* (Wheaton, IL: Tyndale House, 1969).

2. Thomas B. Macaulay, *Critical and Historical Essays Vol. 2, Part III* (New York: A C. Armstrong, 1860), 315.

3. Anonymous.

4. James Conway, *Men in Mid-Life Crisis* (Elgin, IL: David C. Cook, 1978), 57.

5. Norman Cousins, *The Anatomy of an Illness as Perceived by the Patient* (New York: W. W. Norton, 1979), 39–40.
6. Anne Frank, *Anne Frank: The Diary of a Young Girl* (New York: Doubleday, 2001).

Chapter 3: Lonely Singles

1. Ann Kiemel, *I Love the Word Impossible* (Wheaton, IL: Tyndale House, 1976), pp.136–138. Used by permission.
2. *U.S. News and World Report*.
3. *U.S Census Bureau News* "Facts for Features: Unmarried and Single Americans Week," July 19, 2010.
4. Debbie Armstrong, "For Heaven's Sake," *Insight Series ABWE* (Cherry Hill, NJ: Association of Baptists for World Evangelism, 1982), 17. Used by permission.
5. Author Unknown.

Chapter 4: Lonely Spouses

1. "Put Another Log on the Fire," words and music by Shel Silverstein, © 1975 and 1967, Evil Eye Music Company, Inc., New York, NY. Used by permission.
2. Edwin Arlington Robinson, "Richard Cory," *Selected Poems of Edwin Arlington Robinson*, Morton Dauwin Zabel, ed. (New York: Collier, 1965), 9–10. Used by permission.
3. "The Ideal Wife," *A Humorous Look at Love and Marriage*, compiled by Bob Phillips (Eugene, OR: Harvest House, 1981), 54.
4. Tim Timmons, *One Plus One* (Washington, D.C.: Canon Press, 1974).
5. Charles Swindoll, *Strike the Original Match* (Portland, OR: Multnomah Press, 1980), 87.

Chapter 5: Lonely Seniors

1. Margaret Kuhn, *Encyclopedia of 7700 Illustrations*,

compiled by Paul Lee Tan (Rockville, MD: Bible Communications,1979), 931.

2. *U.S. Census Bureau News* "Facts for Features: Older Americans Month," March 23, 2011.

3. Kenneth D. Kochanek, Jiaquan Xu, Sherry L. Murphy, etc. "Deaths: Preliminary Data for 2009," *National Vital Statistics Reports* Vol. 59.4, March 16, 2011, 6.

4. Margaret Kuhn, p.931.

5. Ibid, 931.

6. C. S. Lewis.

7. Anonymous

8. Anonymous

9. Bruce Larson, *There's a Lot More to Health Than Not Being Sick* (Waco, TX: Word, 1981), 75–76.

10. Sherwood Eliot Wirt, *I Don't Know What Old Is But Old Is Older Than Me* (Nashville: Thomas Nelson Publishers, 1992).

11. John E. Roberts, "Now Growing Old," *Encyclopedia of 7700 Illustrations*, 934.

Chapter 6: Lonely Servants

1. William Ramsey, *The Letters to Timothy, Titus, and Philemon*, Revised edition (Philadelphia. PA: Westminster Press, 1975), XIII.

2. Handley C. G. Moule, *The Second Epistle to Timothy, The Devotional Commentary Series* (London: Religious Tract Society, 1905), 16.

3. A. B. Simpson

4. Moule, 158–159.

Chapter 7: Lonely Sufferers

1. Quoted by James L. Johnson, *Loneliness Is Not Forever* (Chicago, IL: Moody, 1979), 151.

2. Johnson, pp. 153–154.

3. Martha Snell Nicholson, *Her Best for the Master* (Chicago: Moody, 1964), quoted by Joyce Landorf, *Mourning Song* (Old Tappan, NJ: Revell, 1974). Used by permission.

4. Charles Swindoll, *Three Steps Forward, Two Steps Back* (New York: Bantam Books, 1982), 19.

Chapter 8: Lonely Survivors

1. Katherine Barrett, "An Epidemic Called Loneliness," Ladies Home Journal, May 1983, 89.

2. Barrett, 90.

3. Carin Rubenstein, quoted by Katherine Barrett, "An Epidemic Called Loneliness," 158.

4. Dietrich Bonhoeffer, quoted by James T. Jeremiah, "Light For Living" Radio Message Series, Cedarville College, Cedarville, Ohio.

Chapter 9: The Lonely Savior

1. Jean-Paul Sartre, quoted by James T. Jeremiah.

2. Robert Ingersoll, quoted by James T. Jeremiah.

3. Keith M. Doornbos, "Never Abandoned," *The Banner*, September 1984.

Chapter 10: Loneliness in the Bible

1. Seneca Epistles, 4.5.

About the Author

Dr. David Jeremiah is senior pastor of Shadow Mountain Community Church in El Cajon, California where he has ministered for more than thirty years. Through his radio and television ministry, *Turning Point*, the Gospel is shared with millions of people every day worldwide. A best-selling author, his books include *Escape the Coming Night, Captured by Grace, Signs of Life, What in the World Is Going On?* and *The Coming Economic Armageddon*.

Dr. Jeremiah and his wife Donna have four grown children and ten grandchildren.

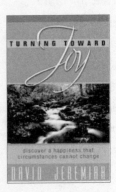
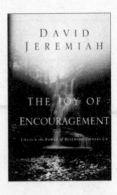

When Your World Falls Apart

When your world falls apart without warning, where is God? Less than a heartbeat away, according to Dr. Jeremiah. Inspired by his own battle with life-threatening illness, *When Your World Falls Apart* is intensely personal as Dr. Jeremiah shares lessons he learned from adversity and the hope he found from the Psalms.

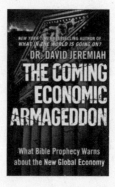

The Coming Economic Armageddon

Today's economy continues to spiral downward and many have compared it to the great depression of the 1930s. Will America be able to recover? Dr. Jeremiah answers this question and more as he examines the current state of the world economy, sets future expectations with prophetic Scripture, highlights current signs that the end is growing closer, and provides biblical principles for meeting upcoming financial challenges.

STAY CONNECTED
TO DR. DAVID JEREMIAH

Take advantage of two great ways to let Dr. David Jeremiah give you spiritual direction every day! Both are absolutely FREE.

Turning Points Magazine and Devotional

Receive Dr. David Jeremiah's monthly magazine, *Turning Points* each month:

- Monthly study focus
- 48 pages of life-changing reading
- Relevant articles
- Special features
- Humor section
- Family section
- Daily devotional readings for each day of the month
- Bible study resource offers
- Live event schedule
- Radio & television information

Your Daily Turning Point E-Devotional

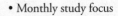

Start your day off right! Find words of inspiration and spiritual motivation waiting for you on your computer every morning! You can receive a daily e-devotion communication from David Jeremiah that will strengthen your walk with God and encourage you to live the authentic Christian life.

There are two easy ways to sign up for these free resources from Turning Point. Visit us online at www.DavidJeremiah.org and select "Subscribe to Daily Devotional by Email" or visit the home page and find Daily Devotional to subscribe to your monthly copy of *Turning Points*.